THE
layman's
guide to
Legal
Survival

ABOUT THE AUTHORS

DAVID SALTMAN is a partner in the firm of Newman, Saltman, Levitt & Feinson, as well as a municipal judge in East Windsor, New Jersey.

GEORGE WILGUS III specializes in personal injury law as a partner in the firm of Lenox, Socey, Wilgus, Formidoni & Casey, and has served as a prosecutor in Mercer County, New Jersey.

THE
layman's
guide to
Legal
Survival

David A. Saltman, J.D., L.L.M. &
George Wilgus III, J.D.

BOB ADAMS, INC.
PUBLISHERS

Published by
Bob Adams, Inc.
840 Summer Street
Boston, MA   02127

ISBN 0-937860-96-4
ISBN 0-937860-95-6 (paperback)

Manufactured in the United States of America.

1 2 3 4 5 6 7 8 9 10
1 2 3 4 5 6 7 8 9 10

Cover design by Giselle de Guzman.

ACKNOWLEDGMENTS

The authors wish to express their gratitude and appreciation to Teri McGee and Doris Sokolove for their unending editorial patience.

Thanks are also in order to: Richard Altman, Esq.; E. John Wherry, Esq.; Elliot Gourvitz, Esq.; the Honorable Leonard Solkolove; Michael Zindler, Esq.; Rudolph A. Socey, Esq.; Dr. Thomas Urbaniak; Adele Lewis; and William Lewis, all of whom shared invaluablke knowledge and experience.

To Brandon Toropov and Bob Adams, the authors extend gratitude for their editorial work and ongoing faith in this project.

Finally, the authors would like to acknowledge those who provided seemingly endless insight into the practical implications of the law as the book was written -- and thus express both love and heartfelt thanks to Robin, Kari, Andy, Jason, and Julie Saltman, and Barbara and Jennifer Wilgus.

DEDICATIONS

This book is dedicated with love to the memory of my mother and father, Fannie "Frankie" Silverman Saltman and Israel Saltman, Esq. I miss them. -- *D.S.*

Dedicated with love to my mother, Serena Wilgus Ashmen and to the memory of my father, George Wilgus. -- *G.W.*

CONTENTS

THE
layman's
guide to
Legal
Survival

INTRODUCTION: THE SIMPLEST RULE FOR LEGAL SURVIVAL

The best advice this book can give is easily boiled down to one concise sentence.

Stay out of court if you possibly can.

Anything can happen in court. The best lawyers will take this crucial point into account when talking to potential litigants, and exhaust every possible avenue for the resolution of a conflict before recommending that a client submit his or her problem to the legal system.

Nevertheless, the odds are that, at some point in our lives, each of us will need the services of an attorney to remedy some unpleasant situation. More often than we might like, that experience may lead us to the courtroom.

And the courtroom, as you'll probably learn from experience, is not for everyone. Furthermore, it's not for every attorney! For those who have no option but to pursue a legal conflict in court, this book offers an "insider's" view of the proceedings that can help you understand what's happening. It also features some pertinent sections on the encounters with "the law" most people must deal with *outside* a courtroom setting: wills, probate, settlement conferences and the like.

The book, however, is not a substitute for an attorney. *The Layman's Guide to Legal Survival* can help you find the *best* attorney, and can help you determine some of the broader questions that may be facing you in your legal dispute or problem. But it will *not* keep you from having to speak with a lawyer in the first place once a real legal problem arises.

"YOU'LL HEAR FROM MY LAWYER!"

A renewed awareness of individual rights and responsibilities has created a lawsuit-happy society, in which, it appears, any slight -- no matter how miniscule -- demands legal retribution.

Lawyers retained, lawsuits filed, the sides square off. What follows, however, is often a study in expense, delay, frustration, deceit, and disillusionment. What at first appeared simple suddenly becomes maddeningly complex.

The client, all too often, blindly relies upon his attorney to "win the case" -- sometimes without even defining exactly what constitutes victory! When difficulties arise, the client blames the high-priced attorney. The lawyer faults an unsophisticated client. Each fails to grasp the fault they share -- a lack of understanding for the multitude of factors that determine the outcome of any lawsuit.

In many instances, the suit's end result has nothing to do with "truth" and "fairness". Rather, the "rules of the game" tend to dictate the outcome. How well does your lawyer play the game? Sometimes it's hard to tell. One thing is certain -- you can't judge your attorney by the standards set on television!

In the real world, the defendant does not confess on the witness stand; the landlord does not admit that an apartment is uninhabitable; the spouse does not agree that he or she was even partially responsible for marital failure.

If you find yourself contemplating or defending a lawsuit, you must try to gain some working knowledge of what takes place inside a courtroom. If you don't, you may miss important opportunities to work with your attorney to minimize losses or take advantage of situations that might work to your benefit.

There are so many questions. Where do you find your lawyer? What do you tell him or her? How do you help make sure your case is a successful one? If you decide to represent yourself, what pitfalls must you avoid?

Regardless of whether your legal difficulty arises from a broken bone, a broken contract, or a broken marriage, there are important factors that you must consider before, during, and after your meetings with any attorney.

Remember: not every dispute requires a lawsuit. Not every problem has a simple solution. Once you enter the legal arena -- the courtroom -- you place your fate in the hands of others. If you must do so, know what you're likely to face.

And then get the most out of your day in court.

CHAPTER ONE:
The Lawyers

THE LAWYERS

What can you expect to encounter in your relationship with a lawyer? How much trust should you place in someone simply because of the fact that he or she is an attorney? Can any attorney handle *your* case?

These are good questions. To most of us, attorneys present a daunting facade. Many people believe that each practicing attorney ends up an omniscient interpreter of the unintelligible; an honest advocate waging tirelessly in the client's best interests at all times; a clever and diligent "inside player" who knows how to make the system work.

The truth is, however, more complicated. Very few new attorneys excel in the most important and elementary institution in the whole of our legal tradition -- the courtroom. Ironically enough, the courtroom happens to be the very spot where the "uninitiated" (read: ordinary people with legal problems) usually need lawyers the most.

In today's complex and increasingly litigious society, almost all of us will at some time see the inside of the courtroom as a participant in the legal process. Unfortunately, few of us will be prepared properly. Even more unfortunately, many of our attorneys will be no better prepared than we are.

This book is a guide to making your way through the legal maze, even if you've never been to law school. It's an aid to determining whether or not your attorney (if you need one at all) knows what he or she is talking about. And it will help you make it through the "system" -- which usually, but not always, means the courtroom -- alive.

WHY YOU MUST BE CAREFUL
IN CHOOSING YOUR LAWYER

Law schools, to begin at the beginning, perform a masterful job of teaching *what* to do, but are a little less than perfect in getting across *how* things get done in the "real world."

Contract, tort, criminal, and constitutional law -- these are some of the fields covered in exhaustive detail. Law schools, however, tend to concentrate on the theoretical aspects of these matters, and not on practical application. While many law schools now have classes in courtroom technique, the law student is often not required to be exposed to an in-depth treatment of the subject.

Certainly the bar exam, which every law student must pass before beginning a professional life as a lawyer, does nothing to bridge the gap between theory and practice. The much-feared test only covers the student's knowledge of legal principles, and does not in any way measure one's capabilities in such areas as rhetorical presentation, one-on-one negotiation, or performance within a hierarchical or bureaucratic structure.

What does all this boil down to? A simple warning: let the buyer beware. The sad fact is, the young lawyer often must "learn the ropes" at the expense of unsuspecting clients. After three years of intensive study, the graduating law student probably has no more knowledge about the workings of the courtroom than the client who'll provide the first dollar earned.

From the first paying client's point of view, there are less expensive ways for an attorney to pick up the most rudimentary courtroom skills in short order. A position with the local Public Defender's or Prosecutor's office is an excellent way for a novice to begin to appreciate the art of "thinking on one's feet." Such a post also allows an attorney to get acquainted with a very important principle, one which, in all likelihood, was not fully covered in law school. Here it is:

The way the facts appear is often more important than the facts themselves.

Law school's theoretical perfection zooms off into the sunset. The new lawyer suddenly must come to grips with a new world, a world where form becomes of greater strategic interest than substance, where practicality outweighs abstract ideas. In the environment of the public defender's or prosecutor's office, a young attorney can learn, within a couple of years, all the elementary requirements of a good trial lawyer. These include the ability to think creatively under pressure, to present what facts are available to the best advantage of the client, and to remain cool even when events take an unexpected turn. All of this can be accomplished in an environment free from the pressures associated with professional trial judgments, open enough to allow constructive criticism from colleagues without affecting one's career prospects, and grounded in the real-life needs of the community for legal service.

Or it can happen at your expense. On your clock. With the outcome of your case in the balance.

Find out about your attorney's background, especially if he or she has not been practicing for long. Don't be cowed by the lawyer's firm, impressive though it may be. Big-city law firms traditionally offer lucrative starting salaries to top-notch prospects fresh out of law school. Unfortunately, those prospects often spend years mired in research tasks at high hourly rates before even *visiting* the courtroom -- which means you may hire someone with "two years of experience" who has as much right to argue your case as someone looking for their first position.

Smaller firms offer a quicker opportunity to gain exposure to the courtroom environment, but frequently fail to provide the intensive, repetitive courtroom experience required to hone skills. The fact to bear in mind is this: there is simply no substitute for getting "into the trenches" and learning first-hand what you can and can't expect to occur as a trial lawyer.

This brings us to another important point. We are, for the moment, discussing trial lawyers -- because courtrooms are the places where, for most of us, the "action" will take place, or threaten to take place. Other lawyers perform in different environments, and other concerns accompany their selection. Many clients, however, will assume that an attorney they've developed a relationship with can handle a divorce or personal injury case as expertly as he or she might, say, draft a will or assist in the sale of a home. It ain't necessarily so.

If you need a lawyer in the medical malpractice field, for instance, you should try to establish a relationship with an attorney who has solid experience in that specialty. Medical malpractice is a field requiring much specific knowledge and experience, and you can't expect someone with a background in probate and nothing but probate to do the job.

Good trial lawyers are made, not born. Their expertise is grounded in hundreds of hours of repetitive witness examination. The courtroom is their battle-ground. It is their home turf. If an inexperienced general practitioner must enter into it, there is no law requiring that you have to be the one paying for it.

That's all very well, you may be thinking to yourself. After all, it only makes sense that attorneys who work regularly in the courtroom are the best people to recruit for a court case. But, for the vast majority of litigants, the question remains: How on earth do I *find* the right person?

FINDING A TRIAL ATTORNEY

Locating a competent trial attorney can be difficult. County and state bar associations will, if you contact them for a suggestion, direct you to the local lawyer referral service in your community. That service will give you a list that purports to outline who does what. But before you dial any numbers, take a hint: the referral service, as a rule, does not screen attorneys in any way. For a fee, a lawyer can be listed in any field of law under the sun.

That's right. If I know next to nothing about divorces, but I ask the referral service to list me as a specialist in divorce settlements, into the list I go as an expert divorce attorney. Provided, of course, that I make out a check for the proper amount.

Basically, the lawyer referral service in your community should be regarded as an advertising arm of the membership -- which brings us to print and broadcast advertising, where the pitfalls are potentially even worse. Suffice to say that, just about anywhere in the country, an attorney can usually say that he or she specializes in any branch of the law -- without a single hour of courtroom experience in that area. Unless the state requires a lawyer to obtain some sort of certification in a given field, advertisements that make such claims are meaningless and yield no information to the potential client.

A note is probably in order here on the subject of state certification. There is a growing trend among many of the state Supreme Courts to implement specific trial certification programs; in such a program, select attorneys are allowed to submit exhaustive trial experience information for review. If the data is verified, the lawyer is permitted to take a written exam on trial procedure and strategy. If he passes the examination, he can advertise that his state's Supreme Court has certified him as a specialist in a given field: say, personal injury, criminal, or matrimonial law. This certification must then be renewed after a given period of years. Information on certified attorneys is available to the public.

Whether or not you come across an advertisement stating that a lawyer is certified, inquire at your local state government information or Supreme Court office about whether your state certifies attorneys. It's an excellent idea to obtain a list of the certified lawyers practicing in your locality.

An advertisement that an attorney is certified should be considered a "green light" in pursuing counsel. Unfortunately, the majority of legal advertising is not as easy for the uninitiated to evaluate. Many attorneys will claim in their ads, for instance, to charge only a "nominal fee for an initial consultation." Again, let the buyer beware. Never forget that successful lawyers are usually good talkers; and good talkers who take out advertisements in order to reach consumers, while they may have law degrees, can also be considered "salesmen." Once you step into the office, there's a pretty good chance that you'll hear more from the salesman than you will from the lawyer. Try to keep in mind that, no matter what you may be told, things are probably neither as simple as they sound nor as complex as they may have been made to appear after that "initial consultation."

Avoid firms that mount expensive media campaigns with the claim that clients "only pay if the attorney recovers an award." Such advertisements, while accurate and within ethical guidelines, only state the obvious, and are an affront to most good trial lawyers. There are virtually no experienced attorneys who will require a fee from an injured party for whom no compensation has been awarded.

If lawyer referral services and advertisements aren't the answer, where *can* you seek assistance?

A local law library is probably the best place to start. Look for a publication called the *Martindale and Hubbell Law Directory.* This resource lists many well-known law firms geographically, and outlines their specialties. Also included are biographical sketches of the firm's partners, associates, and corporate clients.

Like referral services, this resource will list virtually any firm willing to pay the required fee. However -- and this is the crucial difference -- *Martindale-Hubbell does verify the information that appears in its listings.* The book has an excellent reputation, and is used by the country's best law firms when they must refer clients to qualified counsel in another jurisdiction.

Another excellent source is *Best's Dictionary of Recommended Insurance Attorneys.* It is more specialized than Martindale-Hubbell, in that it only lists personal injury attorneys. It includes biographical data and client references. Many insurance companies and corporations consult it when engaging counsel to defend their own interests.

Finally, the American Trial Lawyers Association (ATLA) publishes a directory of its members, who specialize predominantly in criminal, matrimonial, and plaintiff's personal injury matters. This volume, too, should be available at a local law library.

If all else fails, of course, you can always call your county courthouse, determine what day is set aside for civil and criminal motions, and head on down to take a look for yourself. Usually you can hear the oral arguments by opposing counsel in this way. One or two days out of the month will usually be allotted for hearing motions, and while you may not be able to understand the technicalities discussed, you will be able to observe the interaction of the various parties and get a "feel" for who strikes you as most persuasive, best prepared, and most familiar with the system.

Such interplay frequently demonstrates not only a lawyer's capabilities, but also his relationship with the judge hearing the case. Some attorneys -- indeed, some whole firms -- have better relationships with the judiciary than others. Try to narrow down which lawyer seems to have developed a really strong working relationship with His or Her Honor.

As you do so, don't be misled by whether or not an attorney prevails on a given motion. Focus instead on the *way* the judge and the lawyer interact. The dialogue between the two can be very revealing. Remember that even very capable attorneys must at times make less than convincing arguments before the court. How does the judge *respond* to the argument being made? Often a smile or shrug of the shoulders between the court and the attorney will demonstrate that each knows that a position is untenable; sometimes a client must be placated or an argument must be made for the record only. If the judge and the attorney seem to have a good rapport, that can make a difference in a future case.

If you do decide to journey to the local courthouse to hear motions, it would be to your benefit to check the motion lists that normally are posted outside each courtroom. These lists often indicate the type of motion to be heard and, more importantly, the law firms involved. If you see a particular firm's name often, it's a decent bet that it has an extensive and/or well-respected litigation practice.

Obviously, going to the courthouse involves considerable time and effort. And some legal problems will not afford you such a luxury. The field of criminal law, for instance, doesn't always lend itself to long-term, dispassionate analysis. If you are in jail, and you need a lawyer to argue a bail reduction hearing, you can't wander around the courthouse perusing motion lists!

In such a situation, clearly, time is of the essence. The first thing to do is to recognize the fact that you must rely on others to a certain extent. If a friend has engaged a criminal lawyer, try to arrange for that attorney to argue your bail hearing -- then, when things have calmed down a bit, you can think about whom you wish to represent you in the trial itself.

If neither friends nor family have had contact with attorneys who specialize in criminal matters, ask that they contact the local public defender's office for you. Why? Each such office keeps a list of private attorneys for use when conflicts of interest prevent the use of the usual attorneys. These "outside defenders" are frequently former prosecutors or public defenders, and are a fairly solid bet to know all the ground rules of the courtroom in question.

Unless most of your friends are attorneys, you shouldn't lean too heavily on referrals from friends for legal counsel unless you absolutely have to. Most such recommendations are based on subjective impressions of the outcome of a single case. What may have seemed to your friend to be an excellent result may have been only a shadow of what another attorney could have accomplished. *Your* problem, *your* case, and the facts surrounding *your* situation may warrant the use of someone else. Use recommendations from friends as a starting point, but don't depend on them utterly.

If referrals from friends are somewhat suspect, how about newspaper articles extolling the virtues of a particular attorney? Unfortunately, these are often even less reliable indicators. Many columnists write what they are told to (or paid to) write. Certain attorneys court the press shamelessly, providing key facts to a reporter or columnist, who then responds in kind by praising his or her source in print.

Almost every trial lawyer can recount an instance of his adversary's verdict being published in glowing terms, even though the verdict itself might be regarded in professional circles as a less than stellar achievement. Remember, too, that certain cases are "winners" on their own, and require a truly incompetent attorney to have any chance of fouling things up. Suppose you read an enthusiastic article about an attorney who "successfully negotiated a recent personal injury case that resulted in a $2.5 million dollar settlement." Sounds impressive, right? Ask yourself what the facts surrounding the case were, and whether it was the lawyer's competence or the stark nature of the case that was the determining factor. A passenger rendered a quadriplegic by a reckless driver almost certainly will receive a large award regardless of the competence of counsel. Similarly, the published $2.5

million dollar settlement may, in actuality, represent a true cash outlay of only $300,000 or so, accumulating to a larger amount over the life of an annuity.

The point is this: while newspaper articles do shed some light on the legal profession, there is much more going on in any given case behind the scenes than will ever reach the galleys. Don't consider a local write-up gospel until you've been able to do a little investigative journalism of your own.

Once you've used all the sources at your disposal, and you've focused your efforts on a particular attorney, you may hear some talk about an individual's status as a "plaintiff's" or "defendant's" lawyer. Should you worry about this?

In most cases, no. A skilled advocate can handle either end of a case. In fact, he or she often will relish the opportunity to "work the other side of the fence" -- precisely because the prospect of responding to the familiar "tricks of the trade" is an exciting one! The most important thing to look for is the amount of time the attorney has spent in the courtroom -- not the side he or she usually takes.

CHAPTER TWO:
The Rest of the
Courtroom

THE JUDGES

It is amazing, considering the salaries paid, that our judiciary is of such high caliber. Judicial salaries typically fall within the $60,000-$80,000 per year range. Most big-city law firms start their top law school graduates at that level!

Why would an enterprising, intelligent attorney wish to sacrifice income potential to work as a judge? There are several explanations.

First of all, the position is prestigious and powerful. Few other vocations afford a similar opportunity to create social policy, reinforce (or alter) public attitudes, and maintain communal mores -- all with comparatively limited political accountability.

In addition, the judgeship is the highest professional pinnacle that a lawyer can reach. One's self-image, as well as the impression made upon one's peers, can rise considerably during the transition from trial attorney to "your honor".

Finally, the ascension to a judgeship demands the formation of a completely different intellectual perspective. Instead of arguing a particular position, the lawyer-turned-judge must weigh both sides of the case and then proceed to a logically sound disposition of the conflict. Such a task involves a delicate balance between creativity and rational thought -- a balance many attorneys find both stimulating and challenging.

While no one "type" of lawyer aspires to the bench, it

is possible to categorize the successful candidates along broad lines. The first (and worst) category is that of the political crony. Such a judge has received the post he or she holds by paying political dues in one way or another, perhaps by many years of activity in local or national party politics, or even by having mounted actual campaigns for office. Of all judges, the crony is the most feared and loathed by trial attorneys, because the suspicion that political motivations may guide rulings is never completely absent. Friends have placed the crony in the judgeship. Friends may ask for favors in return.

Lawyers usually shun these judges, in large measure because they often possess only borderline qualifications. Occasionally, despite the telltale snickering and unflattering stories in circulation among the trial bar, a crony will, over the passage of time, develop some measure of judicial maturity and experience. By the same token, occasionally he or she continues along the same, more-or-less unqualified lines for a number of taxpayer-subsidized years.

Another category is reserved for the scholar. This is the individual who, perhaps from the very beginning, aspired to become a judge; who relishes reading the law for its own sake; for whom the legal world is work, hobby, and entertainment, all rolled into one.

Such a judge usually works exhaustively, earns respect from all sides, and has a reputation for fairness. Philosophical dispositions may be conservative or liberal, but virtually all of the scholar's decisions are buttressed with ample legal precedent.

Judges such as these, obviously, are considered very

good to work with, because the rules of the game are crystal clear. Any unpleasant surprises that come about in a case are more likely to arise out of one of the attorneys' misunderstanding of precedent or fact, rather than the judge's decision to "change horses in midstream." There can be difficulties, however, associated with cases over which the scholar presides. For instance, scholarly judges who are new to the bench usually will need some time to become truly familiar with practical courtroom procedure, having (usually) reached their positions from the ranks of government or administration within a large law firm.

The older practitioner typifies the third source of judicial talent. Financially comfortable, this judge usually desires nothing more than to distance himself or herself from the chaos associated with the daily practice of law. Having grown weary of dealing with the bewilderingly varied problems voiced by clients, partners, and other participants in the legal system, this judge seeks the refuge of the (supposed) inner calm of the courthouse. No longer must business be solicited, overhead be brought under control, or "emergency" client problems be resolved on short notice. As judge, the older practitioner's effectiveness depends upon diligence, patience, and, to a surprising degree, personality.

The older practitioner relies upon an ability to interact with lawyers that has been developed over a period of years. Such judges usually can grasp practical problems quickly, communicate effectively with all the parties, and help in negotiating settlements that are acceptable to those involved. Among the many tools such a judge can bring to the conflicts to be resolved is a spirit of compromise bred from many years as a member of the bar, as well as an ability to convince others that his or her experience is broad enough to supply real solutions to a wide range of problems. This judge usually understands the importance of "saving face" during a legal conflict, as well.

Finally, we come to the trial lawyer. This is the attorney who has, after a few years of plodding to the courthouse, decided to change gears. This practitioner needs a different type of challenge: after trying enough cases to determine most of the patterns that are likely to emerge, something new is in order. More often than not, such an attorney has been successful financially, and does not need a large income to maintain his or her lifestyle. What makes more sense in this situation, than a judgeship?

Other trial attorneys usually look favorably on the appointment of such an individual -- here, after all, is the perfect judge: someone who knows what it's like to be a lawyer, who hasn't forgotten how it feels to have a witness cancel unexpectedly.

HOW JUDGES SHOULDN'T MAKE IT TO THE BENCH

How does a lawyer become a judge? Basically, there are two ways: election and appointment. Election of judges, though rarer these days, still does occur in many states. Even though some states do incorporate a recall system, the election method is an abominable practice, because it politicizes the judicial system.

Elected judges incur obligation to those who manage their campaigns and donate money. Even with the most scrupulous and honorable judge, there is always a suspicion that, if he or she is elected, the opinions eventually issued may be swayed by partisan politics. Once a judge ascends to the bench, there should be one and only one concern: to administer justice impartially. Other concerns, such as getting re-elected or repaying favors, pollute the process.

Proponents of the election system argue that it guarantees that ineffectual or incompetent judges can be voted out of office. This is not necessarily the case. The general public does not, as a rule, possess the expertise necessary to determine whether or not a judge is competent to hold office. More to the point, the very list from which the public is asked to "choose" is virtually always assembled by a political machine or party, whose motives, as we've seen, often extend beyond the impartial execution of justice. The fact of the matter is, the election process -- by its very nature -- causes judicial candidates to focus on popular causes as political expedients in order to garner votes. There are better ways to select judges.

Appointment based on merit is a much more reliable approach. Under this alternative, a candidate is screened by local and state bar association committees prior to nomination by the state's governor. State police background checks are conducted to probe for any character or emotional deficiencies. Thereafter, legislative committees interview the candidate and eventually vote on the nomination. Under this appointment process, the successful candidate is removed from the most negative influences associated with partisan politics.

What makes a good judge? Consistency and temperament. A judge must be consistent in his or her rulings and procedures. Otherwise trial lawyers will have great difficulty preparing their cases. Most attorneys, actually, will tell you that it's more important for a judge to be consistent than right! After all, if you know someone is dead wrong on a certain issue, you can anticipate ahead of time what you'll have to do to manage the issue. On the other hand, if you *don't know* what to expect, it's very difficult to formulate a realistic strategy.

A strong judicial temperament is a little more difficult to define, but can be equally important. A good judge is diligent, patient, understanding, compassionate, and fair. Arrogance and condescension should not enter into the equation. Unfortunately, there are quite a few judges who view the bench as a rough equivalent to Mt. Olympus. If this is the case, an attorney with a good working relationship with such a judge can be a real advantage.

HOW A JUDGE'S MIND WORKS

How do judges think? Lawyers pray for one who thinks logically. Throughout the course of his or her career, a lawyer is taught to reason logically. One reaches point "C" by proceeding through points "A" and "B", and not by jumping to point "K" and skittering about backwards and sideways. Good judges bring this training with them to the bench. Outlandish arguments or positions are unacceptable, and may not even penetrate the judge's consciousness, even when voiced by the most competent litigator. *Even if they illustrate a valid fact,* illogical or overstated arguments erode a case's validity.

Judges are also taught to rely upon precedent. Legal principles evolve slowly, and the way a case is handled tomorrow depends on the accepted theories of today. Law changes in a step-by-step fashion -- it doesn't leapfrog. As a result, the lawyer who tailors his or her argument to coincide with currently accepted concepts is most likely to gain a sympathetic judicial ear. New and revolutionary readings of old ideas tend to be viewed with skepticism.

A judge need not be a genius. All that's really required is a commitment to reliability and consistency, strong character, and, of course, a willingness to keep abreast of the most recent developments in the law.

A mediocre judge cannot relate to people, but must issue decrees to them. A good judge not only can communicate well, but also understands when negotiations are necessary and under what conditions they will conclude successfully. An excellent judge is one who can negotiate a settlement in which neither side feels that it has lost.

THE JURY

"Voir dire" means "to speak the truth." When lawyers examine prospective jurors, they participate in the "voir dire" process (which can also take place in conjunction with the selection of witnesses). Jurors are selected initially by lot from the public record (usually census, voter registration, or driver's license lists).

Except for grand jury panels, individuals are summoned to serve their county court system as potential jurors for periods normally ranging from one day to three weeks. Grand jury assignments can be longer.

Jurors are assigned to separate groups. When a judge is ready to try a jury case, he or she requests that one or more groups be sent to the courtroom. Thereafter, either the judge or the lawyers query the panels. (Who asks the questions will vary from jurisdiction to jurisdiction; it's a lot more time-consuming when the lawyers are in charge.) Typical questions will concern marital and work status, as well as familiarity with the attorneys, parties, and witnesses. If the issue involves an accident, a juror probably will be asked whether or not he or she ever received a similar injury or was a party to a lawsuit along the lines of the one in question.

After the questioning, the lawyers are allowed to dismiss, or "strike", a number of the jurors without cause. These are called peremptory challenges.

Criminal cases usually require a panel of twelve jurors; civil cases often utilize only six members.

Once the jury is selected, its members are segregated from the balance of the jury panel for the duration of the trial. Unless the case is a very serious criminal matter, the jury is not sequestered overnight. Consequently, most jurors do not have to worry about being cooped up in a hotel room for months on end.

What this means is that if you are on trial, the jurors may be entering and leaving the courtroom every day at the same time you do. Though they are under strict orders, for instance, not to visit an accident scene or converse with the litigants or their attorneys, there is nothing to keep them from observing your mannerisms and decorum. An unintended smirk or ill-tempered gesture made in a courthouse corridor can have as devastating an effect as a blatant misstatement of fact given on the witness stand.

The jury's function is to listen to testimony and to examine the exhibits with open minds before reaching a decision. In most jurisdictions, though it is permissible to request a reading from court transcripts, the jury is not permitted to take notes during the trial. This fact carries tremendous implications. The ways in which testimony and exhibits are presented -- and the degree to which they are memorable -- are just as important as *what* is produced.

Trials usually move forward in bits and pieces. Delays are frequent, because of the difficulty that usually accompanies scheduling doctors, police officers, and other witnesses. Consequently, jurors spend a lot of time in advanced states of boredom.

You and your attorney must make every effort to *interest* the jury in your side of the dispute through the use of visual aids and descriptive devices. Bear in mind that when a jury retires to deliberate. What it does have are the exhibits. That's usually all that can enter the jury room. Consequently, the better the exhibits and the clearer the testimony, the more likely a successful outcome to your case.

SUPPORTING PERSONNEL

Each county judiciary has a supporting administrative staff, responsible for coordinating the processing of civil and criminal cases. This group's most important task is to move cases along as rapidly as possible so as to minimize backlogs. The experienced attorney can use this objective to   advantage in the scheduling of his or her case.

Now to move to the courtroom itself. Who else can you expect to run into besides the judge, the jury, and the lawyers?

Each trial judge works with a stenographer, a bailiff, and a clerk. The stenographer records the testimony, the bailiff keeps order, and the clerk swears in the jury, marks the exhibits for identification, and records the jury's verdict.

Usually, the judge is assisted by a law clerk, typically a recent law school graduate. The law clerk performs much of the legal research for the judge. A judicial clerkship provides the young lawyer with an opportunity to observe the inner workings of the courtroom. This position often serves as a stepping stone to a position with a trial firm, prosecutor's, or public defender's office. Such is the typical makeup of the trial's personnel. In the next chapter, we'll take a look at an encounter that often serves as a litigant's very first step in the legal process: meeting with an attorney.

CHAPTER THREE:
What You Must Tell Your Lawyer -- The First Meeting And Beyond

THE FIRST MEETING

Once you've found the lawyer for your case, what's next?

Your first interview with the attorney is critical for two reasons. As in every important business relationship, the person sitting across the table from you will be judging you not only on what you say, but also on how you say it. Your dress and demeanor are crucial.

Not surprisingly, good lawyers are very sensitive to appearances. They have to be. They earn their living by convincing a judge or jury that their clients' stories are correct. They win cases not only by amassing facts, but also by projecting the facts in an appealing way. *Many more cases are won on appearance than are lost on facts.*

Accordingly, from the moment you walk into his office, your attorney will be viewing your words and actions from the vantage point of a judge and jury. If you talk or dress as though you don't care about the impression you leave, you won't leave a good impression. If you slouch, smoke incessantly, and tap your ashes on the floor, these things will be remembered.

The initial impression, whether you like it or not, will be a lasting one. Try to project yourself as you would like others to see you. You need not wear a three-piece suit, but on the other hand, it's probably not the best idea to walk in soaked in cologne or perfume, or laden with gaudy jewelry.

Remember that when the chips are down, and you're fighting for your money, your name, or your life, you want your attorney to see you as an extension of him or herself -- not some buffoon who probably deserves to be in whatever predicament has surfaced.

Here are some tips that will make the first few minutes you spend with your lawyer work in your favor:

Don't be tardy. Time is money for everyone, but it tends to be more money for lawyers.

An attorney's livelihood is based on billable hours. Late arrivals and unkept appointments create gaps in billable hours and throw delicately arranged schedules off balance. If you know you will be late or will not be able to keep an appointment, call the attorney's office and leave a message to that effect. A simple phone call can keep everyone -- the attorney, other clients, and you -- happy.

Dress cleanly and smartly. Don't arrive in blue jeans, t-shirts, or shorts. Unless you hear otherwise, you can assume that your attorney didn't intend to meet you at the gym.

Lawyers still view their profession as a dignified and honorable one. Remember, too, that the person sitting next to you in the waiting room may be an insurance professional or a bank president. Do not expect an attorney to ignore the possibility that his or her practice may be compromised by your presence. Lawyers thrive on repeat business, and have an image to project to clients and potential clients. If you alienate those clients, you're a liability to the business. That's not how you want to be regarded.

Relax. Engaging an attorney is generally an unpleasant experience. You know it's going to cost you money. The only question is, how much? Getting worked up over fees before fees have been established is, nevertheless, an expensive proposition, because it impedes progress while the "clock" is running.

Financial matters aside, there's usually no shortage of things to be nervous about in the first meeting with your attorney. The only real reason to engage a lawyer in the first place is that you're in trouble or pain -- physical, psychological, or financial. Don't compound the problem by upsetting yourself needlessly. A good attorney will understand your position, having been exposed to it many, many times before. While the facts of your case may be unique, your emotional situation is not.

Do not ramble. Nothing is more disconcerting for an attorney than to listen to a jumbled and haphazard rehashing of one's troubles. Before seeing your lawyer, make a list of the events in question, and order them chronologically. Refer to these notes when telling your story. Do not sermonize. What you believe -- perhaps passionately -- is right or wrong, fair or unfair, pales in comparison with *what actually occurred.* Stick to the facts.

Be prepared. While the primary reason for consulting an attorney is to receive advice and guidance, you'll find that this objective will be compromised if you cannot support important facts with the necessary documents. Without crucial supporting items such as deeds, contracts, and wills, your lawyer will be reluctant to act immediately for fear of compromising your position -- and rightly so.

Of more immediate concern to your finances is the fact that you will extend your visit -- and your legal bill -- if your lawyer must ask you many routine and/or fruitless questions that could be resolved immediately with a quick review of the proper documents.

Listen. A good attorney will play the devil's advocate. Expect to be questioned from your adversary's vantage point. (If you *aren't* questioned from the adversary's point of view, odds are you don't have a very good lawyer!)

The attorney's aim here is not to humiliate you or irritate you, but rather to illuminate all the problems that stand between you and the successful resolution of the case. When your attorney attempts to demonstrate potential difficulties, don't bristle, contradict, or cite irrelevant facts (e.g., "My brother-in-law's bowling partner's aunt's lawyer had a case just like this and won big, quick, so I should too!"). Just listen and provide all the facts you can without getting defensive. This way you'll get a thorough, realistic evaluation of the circumstances surrounding your case. Don't alienate your attorney from doing the job you're paying to have done. He or she may be the only friend you have in the courtroom.

Discuss the fee structure. Yes. Most attorneys recognize that hourly rates between $50 and $500 sound obscene to the average individual. What most people don't realize, however, is that an attorney's hourly rate includes all overhead expenses. Those expenses routinely encompass such costs as secretarial and paralegal help, legal supplies, books, rent, and so on. Normally, these charges account for one-third to a little over half of the hourly rate. The remainder is profit, which often is divided among other attorneys in accordance with a partnership agreement.

Knowing all of this, however, won't do much to ease the awkwardness both you and your attorney may feel when the subject of the cost of his or her services arises. Nevertheless, take the plunge and ask your attorney to estimate the fees you can expect to pay.

Basically, attorneys can bill in one of three ways: per hour, by flat rate, or on contingency. Billing by the hour is the most common method.

When a lawyer bills you by the hour, he or she will record the hours logged on the client's behalf and then bill according to a predetermined rate. In addition to the hourly rate, the client can expect to be billed for other costs such as court filing fees, stenographic bills, and expert witness fees.

In order to protect yourself against sudden changes in your attorney's hourly rate, insist that he or she provide you with a written agreement confirming the arrangement you've entered into.

A flat rate fee arrangement is usually employed when the fees are comparatively small, and will be used most often in traffic, small-claims, and landlord-tenant disputes. In this setting, the lawyer agrees to represent you for a set fee, regardless of the number of hours involved in preparing and presenting your case before the court. Once again, make sure you have written documentation --

a contract -- delineating the agreement.

The third possibility is the contingency fee. This arrangement is common in personal injury cases, and typically involves the injured party engaging counsel on the understanding that the attorney will only receive compensation if the client obtains money in the case. Although rates vary from state to state, the most common scenario will allow the lawyer to deduct one-third of whatever award is realized -- after all costs are deducted.

No matter what form of compensation you settle on, be certain that you understand its format. Commit everything to writing. Don't be bashful about discussing fees with your lawyer. You are paying for services and are entitled to understand how things will be calculated.

Finally – and most important of all – tell the whole truth. Prospective clients often "fudge" the facts in the early stages of the case. This can happen for a number of reasons, including mistrust, fear, and simple embarrassment. Whatever the reasons, and no matter the obstacles, however, it should never happen.

Information you impart to your attorney is *completely confidential*, and, under our nation's concept of jurisprudence, is protected by the attorney-client privilege. This relationship precludes your lawyer from revealing your confidences without your permission. Should your attorney make the ethically indefensible, *extremely* rare and professionally suicidal decision to divulge such secrets, they could not be used against you in court, and could form the basis for a viable suit for damages against the attorney.

If you are charged with a crime, for example, and

consult an attorney for advice, the lawyer *cannot* provide the police with any information he or she receives from you on your role in the crime -- *even if you admit complete responsibility to the lawyer.* Attorney-client privilege, of course, is not limited to criminal matters; it applies to everything you disclose to the lawyer, whether the information is criminal, civil, or matrimonial in nature.

Nevertheless, many clients will hesitate before recounting the full background of the difficulty in which they find themselves. This is especially true in matters such as divorce litigation, where the prospect of having compromising personal information examined openly is not usually greeted with much enthusiasm. If you fail to give all the facts to your lawyer, however, you are cheating yourself. You can rest assured that if you can recall all of the incidents surrounding the conflict, your spouse or adversary can, too. It's better for your attorney to know the full set of facts from the very beginning than to be taken by surprise as you're being cross-examined by your opponent's counsel. If your case ends up in the latter category, you won't need a lawyer anymore. You'll need a miracle.

Understand that attorneys face unpleasant situations daily. As long as your lawyer knows about the weaknesses in your case from the beginning, he or she can *compensate* for them and minimize their impact. But if the information doesn't surface until halfway through the process, or surfaces under less-than-perfect circumstances, you'll be in trouble. Tell the whole truth from the start.

If, for example, you've been squirrelling away most of your assets without informing your spouse, take a moment to enlighten the attorney who's handling your divorce. If you do, you can be sure your case will pursued along the correct strategic lines (in this case, settling out of court quickly, because all the salient facts have a habit of rising to the surface in a contested divorce). If you don't, you may spend quite a lot of time pursuing a path your lawyer thinks is correct, but isn't. As if that weren't bad enough, you could spend some time in jail for lying about your assets.

If you still feel reticent about examining all the facts with your lawyer, bear this in mind: judges are, on occasion, lenient with burglars, embezzlers, or child molesters, but they tend to take a *very* dim view of perjurers. Talk openly with your lawyer about all the aspects of your case; don't fool yourself into believing you can "wing it" on the stand or in a deposition. Get everything out on the table so the right strategy -- which is, after all, what you're paying the lawyer to come up with -- accompanies your case.

OTHER TIPS THAT WILL MAKE THE FIRST MEETING RUN SMOOTHLY

Bring a pen and a pad of paper with you. Your attorney will indicate what additional information he or she needs. Write it down so you have a permanent record of what is required and can provide it as quickly as possible. When forwarding the requested information, keep copies for yourself to safeguard against a loss in transit.

When important documents such as financial ledgers, deeds, or wills are sought, be sure to ask whether you are being asked to provide the originals. If you are, make every attempt to deliver them by hand, rather than trust them to a third party. If this is impossible, send the items by certified mail.

Make every attempt to adhere to the schedule set out by your attorney. If your lawyer specifies a deadline for, say, completing a list of written questions (otherwise known as "interrogatories") don't treat the deadline frivilously. It was set for a reason. Failure to comply with your responsibilities as a litigant can result in a weakened position, monetary fines, or even the dismissal of your case.

GETTING TO SPECIFICS

The guidelines above reflect broad approaches to the best way to begin the attorney-client relationship. What follows are more specific suggestions for those involved in a number of the most common legal problems. You will probably want to examine those that most nearly approximate your situation before you visit your lawyer for the first time.

PERSONAL INJURY

If you have been involved in an accident, whether as victim, wrongdoer, or simply confused participant, compile a list of the names, addresses, and daytime and evening phone numbers of all possible witnesses. Indicate the date, time, and place of the incident. Continue by specifying as many details as possible: describe the weather conditions, degree of illumination, and presence or absence of obstructions that may have impeded vision. If possible, collect copies of all police, fire, or other investigatory reports prepared by municipal officials as a result of the event. Obtain color photographs of the scene as quickly as possible, being certain to include in the picture any machines involved in the accident (for instance, damaged cars, ladders, cranes, etc.).

While instant cameras have obvious advantages, they can create color and lighting distortions. If at all possible, take both instant color and 35mm photographs. If the incident occurred at night, take photographs depicting, as accurately as possible, the scene both in daylight and in darkness.

Prepare a complete narrative outlining how the incident unfolded. Be sure to include the substance of all relevant conversations that took place. If the witnesses are cooperative, request that they give you a written note or statement of what happened. Make certain that they sign the note or statement, so that it can be used as evidence should they attempt to alter their description of events at a later date. This description also can be used to refresh someone's memory, if there is a genuine memory lapse after a few months or so.

If you were injured, gather a copy of the emergency room report or other applicable documentation. Secure copies of all medical records that pertain to any hospital stays. These records routinely include the admission history, initial physical examination, progress notes, consultation reports, x-rays and laboratory study reports, diagnostic test reports, and discharge summary.

You also should get the names, addresses, and office phone numbers of all the physicians who treated you as a result of the accident. Your lawyer will have you sign a medical release form to facilitate the acquisition of follow-up reports and prognoses.

Write the names, addresses, and daytime and evening phone numbers of those friends, neighbors, relatives, fellow employees, and employers who were familiar with your health and appearance before the accident, and who would be willing to relate, if necessary, how the incident may have altered your appearance or performance in their eyes. If time permits, seek their permission before visiting your attorney. (If, however, this topic is something that you find difficult to discuss, delegate the task to your lawyer.)

Itemize all the bills, charges, expenses, and financial losses you have sustained because of the accident. List the name, policy number, and claim numbers of all liability and health insurance policies that were in effect at the time of the accident. Take those policies to your attorney's office, with photocopies that he or she can keep.

Finally, be sure to provide your lawyer with your address and daytime and evening phone numbers. You should describe briefly your educational background, indicating all prizes or awards that you may have received. Specify any organizations in which you're active, and outline your hobbies and outside activities -- being sure to specify those that have been affected due to injuries resulting from the accident. You also should identify in writing all other prior and subsequent accidents and injuries, and give a detailed account of your employment background.

MATRIMONIAL MATTERS

Though it may seem to you to be an impossible task, prepare a detailed narrative outlining all present and past difficulties you have encountered with your spouse. Mention not only those difficulties for which you feel your spouse should shoulder responsibility, but also those elements of the marriage in which you may have fallen short. It will be difficult to provide any appraisal of personal problems, but you must attempt to provide your lawyer with all the facts. Remember that any unpleasant fact you conceal is very likely to be raised by the opposition. If your lawyer is going to hear about some indiscretion eventually, you might as well get it out in the open now. Make every effort to provide a detailed history of the marriage that incorporates all the facts, especially if you foresee any possibility of a custody battle.

Past histories become very important when the court must determine custody questions.

List your income and your spouse's income for the year past. This income, of course, will include all money earned from employment, together with any funds realized in the form of interest, dividends, capital gains, or related sources. By referring to your joint income tax returns, you can simplify this task. In fact, when you visit your attorney, you should provide, if at all possible, all returns, joint or separate, for the last five years. The information on these documents will enable the attorney to formulate a clear picture of your financial situation.

Outline all of your joint assets, specifying the name, amount, and value of all stocks, bonds, mutual funds, or governmental securities owned either jointly or individually. You can check the financial section of your newspaper for the present value of the asset, if necessary.

Be sure to account for your real estate, indicating its location, purchase price, mortgage amount, and present value. If you have no idea of the property's present value, you should specify its assessed value for municipal tax purposes.

Make note, as well, of any pension plans, annuities, stock options, or life insurance that you or your spouse may own.

It isn't necessary to enumerate household items and their values, though you should specify any objects you consider unique or of special monetary value.

Specify all of your joint and separate debts and standard expenditures. Because most of the payments on these debts occur monthly, list the monthly payment due where appropriate. For those expenditures which don't take place regularly, but are essential to your living standards (for example, clothes), calculate what you spend over a year, then divide that figure by twelve. Conversely, for those charges that occur weekly, multiply the figure by 4.3 to determine the monthly rate.

Some states will require that all matrimonial litigants complete a preliminary financial disclosure statement, which will require detailed financial information along the lines of the data outlined above. Whether your state requires such information or not, you and your lawyer should be familiar with the figures involved. They are integral elements of a divorce case, and foundations to the successful resolution of alimony, child support, and property distribution questions.

COMMERCIAL MATTERS

The first thing an attorney will ask about, in the vast majority of all commercial cases, is the contract involved in the dispute. Be sure to bring it to the attorney's office the very first time you meet with him or her.

Because contracts often are modified by later writings between the parties involved, you should also provide your lawyer with copies of all relevant letters, memoranda, phone messages, or other correspondence. Equally important are any letters or documents exchanged between the parties before the contract was signed. Be sure your lawyer has access to all relevant items that may help resolve ambiguities or define contested language.

If you are involved in a conflict over an oral agreement, gather whatever documentation you have which may confirm that agreement. Usually you will have none. This problem highlights one of the chief difficulties associated with entering into oral agreements. If you are *very* lucky, the other party may have taken some inadvertent action that will convince the court that you are entitled to some reimbursement as a matter of fairness. (*Note:* Unless you consider yourself an astoundingly lucky person, do not rely on oral agreements for anything. If you insist on doing so, be prepared for the worst if there is a disagreement somewhere down the line.)

CHAPTER FOUR:
The Pros and Cons of Shouting "Sue Them!"

"SUE THEM!"

They welched on the contract! There's no doctor on earth who would have done that! They won't refund the money! Quick! Call the lawyer!

Every wrong, it sometimes seems, deserves and demands a right. In order to set things straight, you have to call a lawyer, who has to initiate a law suit. That'll show 'em.

Or will it?

Sometimes plunging headlong into the legal abyss can have dire and expensive consequences. In this chapter, we'll try to outline the trickier aspects of pursuing a court action against someone you feel has wronged you. With a working knowledge of the principal problems you'll encounter, you'll find yourself in a much better position to make decisions.

The fact of the matter is, you *do* have important decisions to make. The very first one, thankfully, is an easy one. You must decide *not to decide anything* while you are sitting in the attorney's office.

A decision to sue someone should be based on many considerations -- not merely your belief that an enemy "has it coming." Too many suits are initiated in the heat of the moment, or "manufactured" by unscrupulous attorneys who need business.

What should you do in your first meeting with an attorney advising you on whether or not to pursue a lawsuit? Ask questions. Listen to the answers. Write the answers down. And don't let yourself get talked into anything.

It's such an important point it bears repeating. *Do not decide anything* -- pro or con -- with regard to pursuing the lawsuit until you have left the attorney's office and had some time to review the facts on your own.

That having been said, let's examine some of the basic questions you should make sure your attorney addresses in that first meeting. Whether your conflict involves a divorce, a criminal matter, a bankruptcy, or some other matter, the following queries are important benchmarks that will help you determine the "winnability" of the case.

QUESTIONS YOU SHOULD ASK YOUR LAWYER:

Do you think I can win or make an attractive settlement? What compensation can I realistically expect from this case? What is the likelihood of settling out of court? Determining the "bottom line" is important. If you don't ask the right questions, you can be in for some unpleasant surprises as the case progresses. If you were in an automobile accident and broke your finger, you may feel that you have a case against the person you feel was at fault in the incident. Your appraisal of the matter may be that you have approximately $100,000 coming. If you're lucky, you'll find out from your lawyer that the circumstances of the case indicate that you will be determined to have partial responsibility for the accident. Add the facts that the break was not serious and that you recovered fully, and you could be looking at the princely sum of $1000 in a good case scenario. Deduct the attorney's fees and related costs, and guess what? Your net recovery is perhaps five hundred dollars, which you probably could have picked up in a couple of weeks tending the counter at your local Burger King -- with considerably less aggravation and inconvenience. By the same token, an injury you've undergone may be worth considerably more than you think. A good lawyer will be able to recognize the potential of your case and summarize it intelligently for you.

If you don't feel comfortable making an estimate as to what I could be awarded, would you specify a potential range into which this case's compensation might fall? It is a common occurrence for an attorney to be unable to give you an exact dollar evaluation of a case. Nevertheless, some type of range should be possible to formulate.

Why does this compensation seem so (high) (low)? If the figures cited sound very high, the attorney may be raising your hopes unrealistically in the hopes of generating some "easy" billable hours. If the figures sound unrealistically low, he or she may be attempting to trick you into believing the case's position is worse than it actually is -- so you'll be all the more impressed at the eventual "big" victory and come back as a repeat customer.

What specific amount would you recommend suing for? Why? If the answer is less than you had in mind, remember: there's no such thing as a perfect case. By the same token, if you get signals that the lawyer is unenthusiastic about pursuing the case, you've got two options: give up, or get another opinion from someone else. Whatever you do, don't trust your case to a lawyer who thinks the case is not worth pursuing! Even if your attorney is competent during the trial, you may miss out on a settlement -- opposition lawyers usually can sense when someone expects to lose, and will hold off on making you an attractive offer.

How will you charge me? Will there be a contingency arrangement? Or are you planning on charging an hourly rate? If you are charging on a contingency basis, what percentage will you retain and how will you determine the final figures you'll be using? If you are charging on an hourly basis, what is your hourly rate? Can we combine the two payment methods somehow, combining a lower hourly rate with an adjusted contingency arrangement? Although it isn't "standard operating procedure," there's a good chance that you can make an arrangement with an attorney for a partial hourly fee and a partial contingency fee. In this scenario, you would agree to pay one-half of the attorney's hourly rate for each hour put into the case. (The total amount of money paid in this way would be computed as part of the normal contingency arrangement, should the attorney make a recovery on your behalf.) The advantage to this system is that he or she has an incentive to work on your case for a large award, while you are spared the aggravation of paying full-scale fees for a case you don't win. Though the arrangement is not a typical one, there are usually no reasons for an attorney to turn down such a suggestion. Obviously, this scenario is most attractive from your point of view if you're in a situation in which you would otherwise pay your attorney by the hour.

What is the likelihood of losing this case? Most people wouldn't try to initiate a lawsuit they consider unwinnable. However, you can expect a good lawyer to look at your case with a greater degree of objectivity than you can. Try to get the most honest appraisal of your legal position possible, and don't be insulted if the lawyer tells you the odds aren't in your favor. *Remember: you aren't making a decision yet.* You're gathering facts.

Will I have to pay the other side's attorney's fees if I lose? Some states will hold you responsible for attorney fees and court costs if you bring a suit which you subsequently lose. These costs should be considered in any evaluation of a case

Are any experts necessary for a successful outcome? If so, what costs are involved? How must payments be made to these individuals? The cost for an expert's time to, say, write a report, can range from $100 to $500 per hour. An average number of hours of pretrial work would probably fall somewhere between five and fifteen. These costs add up. Make sure you know what the costs are likely to be -- ahead of time. If you're talking about spending $1500 in expert witness fees to pursue a $5000 award, you need to review the case closely -- and perhaps consider an offer from the other side to settle for $4000 before spending the $1500.

How long do you estimate it will take for this case to be resolved? How long will it take to get a trial date? Will there be depositions? Interrogatories? Testimony? Virtually every well-litigated case will require considerable pretrial work and, from the point of view of many litigants, seemingly unreasonable delays. These are factors frequently overlooked in the process of deciding whether or not to sue. Be sure you have a good idea of exactly what schedule you can expect to incorporate.

Why are you qualified to take this case? What other cases have you handled along these lines? What were their outcomes? This may be difficult to ask. Do it anyway -- tactfully. Perhaps the most important questions you'll be asking are the ones that give you an idea of the attorney's competence in the field of law your case falls in. Unless you are dealing with a lawyer you can depend on utterly (for instance, an old family friend) don't expect someone to leap up and tell you that they're unqualified to handle your case. As we pointed out earlier, there are lawyers, and there are courtroom lawyers. Even if your attorney has worked successfully with you on a non-trial matter such as a will, do not assume he or she is experienced enough to handle a personal injury case. A lawyer who specializes in complex wills only, but tells you he can handle your accident case probably has decided to embark on some on-the-job training at your expense. To be sure, there are many attorneys who do specialize in many fields and perform fantastically at each. The key is to try to pin down past experiences in your area of interest. If you can't do that, you'll be depending on locating the honest attorney -- the one who'll tell you, "Listen; I don't do much work in this area, but I can refer you to someone who does." They're out there, but you shouldn't assume you've run into one unless you see proof.

Will you be handling this case personally? If not, why not? It is not unusual for attorneys in medium- to large-sized firms to do the "front" (i.e., appearing in court) work on a case, and then refer the matter to an associate for the paperwork and other details of varying importance. The attorney you initially meet with may not even be the person who appears in court! Obviously, it's preferable to have the person you discuss your case with be the one making the presentation to the judge or jury, the one filing pleadings, handling depositions, issuing motions, and coordinating all the other details of your case. A good fee arrangement should incorporate accurate rates of all the people involved in your case.

What obstacles have to be overcome in my case? How will we do this? Even if your case may be solid as far as facts are concerned, there are certain intangibles that must be taken into account. If you're suing a sweet, lovable widow who stands four feet eleven inches tall and offers to make cookies for everyone she comes in contact with -- including your lawyer -- you may have some problems. *Remember, there is no such thing as a perfect case.*

Who will rule on this case – a judge or a jury? If a judge, do you have any idea who might be assigned this case? Some judges have reputations for being a "plaintiff's judge" or a "defendant's judge." Some have reputations for being sympathetic to men, others to women. Some are simply known for their fairness. Any capable attorney can advise you as to what judges might hear the case -- and also can give you insights as to whether or not your case is better off in front of a jury than a judge.

What effect would pursuing this case have on my (job) (family life) (reputation) (sanity)? Would any publicity – positive or negative – be generated by this case? What, in your judgment, would be the long-term effects of such publicity? Any publicity which may be generated by the filing of certain actions, whether justifiable or not, could cause a potential employer to reject your application for employment. Similar problems may arise with reference to your personal reputation or relationships with others. Although most lawsuits receive little, if any, publicity, the potential for future problems is real. Many attorneys fail to bring this to the attention of their clients. Similar difficulties may arise with reference to your personal reputation or relationships with others.

If the above seems like a lot to ask -- it is. But bear one thing in mind: the first meeting is the meeting you get to use to gather information. That's why you're paying the lawyer to sit there and talk to you. Don't be shy. Get your money's worth. Ask the questions.

CHAPTER FIVE:
The Courthouse
Steps -- Methods
and Procedures

COPING WITH THE WORK
BEFORE THE VERDICT

Most attorneys, sad to say, are either too busy or too oblivious to advise clients of the method in which their clients' problems ultimately will be addressed in court. Consequently, very few people possess even a rudimentary understanding of the procedural steps associated with their case -- and develop understandable feelings of confusion, anxiety, and bitterness about "the system" and how it is affecting their lives.

This chapter is dedicated to the simplification of the stages common to each and every lawsuit, from the initial filing to the final verdict. Armed with this knowledge, even a client with no legal inclinations whatsoever can cope more successfully with the complex and demanding procedural nature of our legal system.

You may wish to consult the Appendix of this book for some samples of various documents and related items you'll find discussed in this chapter.

THE COMPLAINT

The first step in any lawsuit is the filing of the *complaint*. What is a complaint?

Basically, a complaint lists the person initiating the action as the *plaintiff*, and identifies the person against whom the suit is brought as the *defendant*. More importantly, it states the plaintiff's position with regard to the conflict. Together, the plaintiff(s) and defendant(s) are be referred to as the *litigants*, or *parties*. The complaint is usually filed in a central court office location, which keeps copies of all relevant records.

In addition to specifying the names of the litigants and outlining the conflict from the plaintiff's point of view, the complaint also states the name of the court where the suit will be argued, the relevant division of that court, and the county where the court is located.

The *body* of the complaint lists the name and address of the plaintiff, and proceeds to furnish basic information necessary to establish the basis for the suit against the defendant. Due to space constraints, the complaint sometimes only relates a brief summary of the incident or incidents, but gives the court a clear and vigorous description of the events in question.

A complaint usually will be accompanied by a *summons* when it's presented to the defendant. This is simply legal notice to the defendant that the complaint has been filed, and that a response is required. Also specified is the number of days within which the defendant must file an answer to the complaint, and directions as to where that answer should be sent.

THE ANSWER

When a complaint is filed by the plaintiff's side, the defendant usually will respond by filing an *answer*. (In some small claims, tenancy, and criminal matters, this isn't necessary. These cases will be discussed in a little more detail later on in the book.)

An answer is usually a response to key points in the complaint. In the answer, a defendant may admit some participation in the incident in question, but deny negligence. The answer may also contain what are referred to as *separate defenses*, outlining the different specific claims of the accused person. These typically introduce new elements to the dispute arising out of the complaint. Different states have different requirements regarding defenses which must be raised in an answer. Often, if a defense is not set forth in an answer, it may not be used at a later date.

Separate defenses, are, like the complaint, short and sweet. They clearly indicate why the defendant should not be considered responsible for the incident specified in the complaint. The defenses vary with the type of complaint being filed and the matter in dispute.

CROSSCLAIMS AND COUNTERCLAIMS

If there are multiple defendants, one common procedure is for one defendant to make a *crossclaim,* or claim against one or more of the other defendants. What this really means is that Defendant A is saying the incident in question is the responsibility of Defendant B.

A *counterclaim* also may be asserted by any of the defendants against the plaintiff. A counterclaim is very similar to a complaint, in that it sets forth the basic facts necessary to establish a conflict the court must resolve. However, the person who must undergo scrutiny now is the plaintiff.

THIRD- (AND FOURTH- AND FIFTH- AND SIXTH-...) PARTY COMPLAINTS

A *third-party complaint* is a complaint (generally filed with the answer, crossclaim, and counterclaim, by the defendant) against someone not already a litigant in the suit. This, too, contains basic information and allegations against an individual who, the defendant claims, had some hand in the incident in question.

Here and in the counterclaim, the terminology can get a little confusing. In most cases, the defendant (or person answering a complaint) will be the one who *initiates* a third-party (or fourth- or fifth-party, for that matter) complaint -- becoming, in effect, a plaintiff, right?

So we refer to Defendant A, once he or she has filed a third-party complaint, as the *third-party plaintiff* -- even though, as far as the original complaint is concerned, Defendant A still remains the defendant. We refer to the person Defendant A identifies and files a third-party complaint against as the *third-party defendant.*

If you think that's confusing, watch what happens when the third-party defendant decides someone *else* should be considered entirely responsible, and files a *fourth-party complaint,* thereby becoming the *fourth-party plaintiff.* This brings a *fourth-party defendant* into the fray, of course, who is then entitled to file a *fifth-party...*

You get the idea. Theoretically, this type of complaining against additional parties could go on forever. Broadly speaking, such complaints are more the exception than the rule.

INTERROGATORIES

Once all of the complaints, answers, crossclaims, and third-party complaints have been filed (usually under strict deadlines), we're ready to move on to the real work that must be done in any suit.

Interrogatories are written questions posed by one side for the other to answer under oath. These questions will be an integral part of virtually every legal action.

Obviously, the content of these questions will vary from case to case and from state to state, but they must, as a general rule, be submitted and answered between thirty and one hundred eighty days from the beginning of the case.   Failure to answer interrogatories can carry heavy penalties.   Failure on the part of your lawyer to file interrogatories for the other side to respond to would give you a pretty decent shot at a malpractice case against your attorney.

It's always a good idea to review with your lawyer the answers the other side has given.   Doing so will give you a good idea of the story the jury or judge will be facing, and may shed some more light on your attorney's overall strategy.

DEPOSITIONS

A *deposition* is a question and answer period which takes place under oath for admission to the record. Over the course of the interview, a qualified stenographer will take down all that is said.   Depositions usually take place in the offices of one of the attorneys; it is not necessary that they be conducted in the courthouse.

During a deposition, you will be questioned by the opposition's attorney, though your lawyer can, as a rule, interject clarifying comments or request that an issue or question be restated for you.   There is very little that cannot be asked at a deposition; as long as the question has some relevance to the case and is not subject to privilege (for instance, that between an attorney and a client), a lawyer can feel free to pose it without fear of being overruled or censured.   Witnesses can also be deposed.

The atmosphere at a deposition is generally informal, but don't let that fool you. Remember that all the answers you give are under oath. Remember that the opposing attorney is not your best buddy. Each lawyer enters into this process with the objectives of learning your position in the conflict and obtaining a written record they can use to *win the case.* If the other side wins, you lose. Don't "let it it all hang out"; keep a close eye on your attorney throughout the deposition, and monitor his or her reactions to the questions posed.

Some cases (where there is not a great deal of money at stake) can be waged successfully without depositions. This is an important consideration, as long, drawn-out depositions mean lots of billable attorney's hours. If you are engaged in a comparatively modest-sized case, be sure to review with your lawyer the possibility of managing the financial end of the case more effectively by dispensing with this step.

DEMANDS FOR ADMISSIONS

Demands for admissions are requests for information by an attorney of the opposition litigants, usually requiring a "yes or no" type answer. These demands are generally used in contract cases; however, they can be employed in other cases as well.

The deadline for responding to demands for admissions is usually much briefer than that for interrogatories, and the answers, of course, must be definitive ones.

EXAMINATIONS

Examinations take many forms. If the case is a malpractice or negligence matter, examinations are usually conducted by a doctor on behalf of one of the litigants. This doctor will render an opinion as to what is wrong (or not wrong) with the plaintiff, and furnish the court with a prognosis regarding the extent of damage to the plaintiff.

In other cases, examinations may also take the form of a visit to the scene of an accident: perhaps a street, subway, or factory. Examinations also can allow the judge or jury to get a first-hand look at any of the items or relevant documents associated with the event in dispute: for instance, a car, bus, or purportedly defective machine.

DEMANDS FOR ADMISSION
AND NOTICES TO PRODUCE

A *demand for admission* is a query made by one party upon the other to admit that certain facts are true. If your adversary admits the facts in question -- or fails to respond within a certain period -- the facts are treated by the court as being true. (Obviously, this is an important point to bear in mind if you are the one being served with the demand for admission.)

Your lawyer may serve your opponent with a demand for admission in the hope that the facts in question will be conceded. By eliminating opposition to as many facts as possible, your lawyer can streamline your case, thereby permitting the judge or jury to concentrate on the issues most important to your case.

A similar tool is the *notice to produce.* As you may remember, this is a request to inspect items critical to the case, such as documents, products, or machinery in the possession of your adversary. This request also may include a notice to enter land or buildings for the purpose of surveying, inspecting, measuring, or photographing the property or some item contained in it.

Lawyers usually will honor these notices, with two major exceptions. The first is a request for materials that contain proprietary or trade secret materials; and the second is the instance that requires some destructive testing of the item. In either situation, the court can establish guidelines that will protect all litigants.

If your lawyer forwards a notice to produce to you, it's crucial that you come forth with any difficulties you might incur by complying. Don't wait until the last moment to raise such issues; the earlier you advise your attorney of your concern, the more effectively he or she can respond to limit any damaging consequences.

MOTIONS TO COMPEL DISCOVERY

Motions to compel discovery represent a solution the courts have instituted for getting litigants to comply with reasonable requests for discovery by the opposition. Without these motions, cases could drag on endlessly.

If Mr. Smith and Miss Jones, for instance, are involved in an automobile accident, it may be very important to determine exactly how the accident occurred. Perhaps the case could turn on the issue of whether Mr. Smith sustained damages on the right or left side of his car. Perhaps Mr. Smith's attorney knows that revealing the fact that the auto -- still in Mr. Smith's possession -- is in fact scraped up on the left hand side will damage Mr. Smith's case. What's the lawyer's first instinct? Stall.

But Miss Jones and her attorney want to see the car. Nevertheless, all the attorney's requests and the judge's instructions have been met with delay after delay. A motion to compel discovery is made, and the judge issues an order to compel that discovery -- in other words, he or she orders Mr. Smith and his attorney to allow the car to be examined, because a review of the physical condition of the car represents a reasonable request on the part of Miss Jones' attorney.

Obviously, failing to comply with such an order is not a good idea. Not only could Mr. Smith's case be dismissed, he could face monetary fines or even, if the violation is a flagrant one, a jail sentence.

SETTLEMENT CONFERENCES

It should come as no surprise that not all cases are argued all the way through to a final verdict from the judge or jury. The elaborate bargaining, re-evaluating, and brinksmanship that accompanies the final stages of many cases frequently results in a settlement; and the formal environment in which the negotiations take place is known as the *settlement conference*.

There are generally three types of settlement conferences. The first takes place among the lawyers themselves; the second, also referred to as an early settlement conference or panel, involves another party (usually another lawyer) acting as an arbitrator; and the third takes place in the presence of the judge.

Settlement conferences can take place at any point in the case. In the first instance cited above, one attorney could merely call the other's office and ask what it would take to settle the case being argued; each lawyer might then sit down and pass along the relevant information to the client or clients, discuss the issues, and see what happens. Certainly, from the client's point of view, this approach is attractive: it's cheap, easy, comparatively convenient, and, assuming the case is not a bitterly contested one, fairly likely to yield a satisfactory outcome. There is one potential difficulty: this method can tend to drag on for a while, as there is no real pressure on any of the litigants to settle (or decide against settling) from the court itself.

An early settlement conference, the second type of meeting, usually is court-ordered. It customarily takes place in the presence of arbitrators, typically lawyers familiar with the type of case being argued. These panel members will hear from both sides and then make "suggestions" as to how the case could be settled. Such suggestions tend to carry quite a bit of weight, and a large percentage of the cases reaching this environment are settled.

Why? There are several reasons. Litigants get to hear the other side of the case in some detail -- perhaps for the first time truly realizing that their position could conceivably have some weaknesses. In addition, there is a tendency to trust that the members of the panel know what they're doing when they make a suggestion, and that a judge or jury is very likely to view the case from the same perspective that the panel takes. Finally, because the proceedings are court-ordered, they take place at the courthouse. Though an informal atmosphere may be the norm, the conclusions reached there carry a certain sense of authority. Even though the determinations are not imposed upon the participants, the insights of the panelists, though regarded as suggestions, are usually accorded considerable respect.

If the suggestions of an objective panel are viewed with a healthy sense of pragmatism, you can imagine what happens when the person handing down the suggestions is the judge who'll be trying the case! That's the setting for the conference with the judge, our third option, which is, actually a very simple affair. The attorneys for all parties meet for the purpose of making a presentation to the judge of the merits of deciding in their favor. The judge will give his or her evaluation, which will not only carry quite a bit of weight, but will also put considerable pressure on the parties involved to settle quickly. Sometimes a litigant will hear his attorney sum up a complex, involved, and emotionally difficult case with surprising brusqueness: "The judge thinks the case is worth..."

Sometimes, hard as it may be to accept, a complicated question has a simple answer.

CHAPTER SIX:
How To Win
Points --
Before Trial

DISCOVERY

The experienced lawyer knows that most civil lawsuits are won or lost before the trial begins. Many months before the first courtroom appearances, the well-versed trial lawyer will have planted the seeds of victory during the discovery process.

During this process, opposing sides test the strengths and weaknesses of each other's position. Typically, an attorney will use all the available outlets for information -- depositions, interrogatories, and the rest -- to ferret out data that will present the client's case in the most favorable light, and discredit positions adopted by the other side.

In this chapter, we'll be examining the best strategies you and your lawyer can employ to make sure that the pretrial period -- which is, in many cases, the only period that matters -- yields a successful outcome to your case.

INTERROGATORIES: YOUR CASE ON PAPER

As discussed earlier, interrogatories are typed questions served by each side of the conflict. Your lawyer must prepare interrogatories for your opponent, and you must answer interrogatories from your opponent's counsel.

You should have some idea of what will be required before you attempt to complete your interrogatory. If you have engaged expert witnesses, you will be required to state the substance of their oral reports; you may also have to produce copies of the experts' written opinions and give documentation on their background.

Most importantly, of course, you'll be required to state the facts upon which you will be relying in arguing the merits of your case. Remember that while one purpose of an interrogatory is to shed light on the facts of the case, another function is to pin down your position in the conflict.

As you might imagine, careless or inaccurate interrogatory responses can be devastating at trial. Your opponent can -- and surely will -- cite your responses from the interrogatory if they show the least variance from your courtroom statements. Such discrepancies (which may seem innocent enough at first) are exploited routinely in jury trials to impeach a litigant's credibility.

The best overall advice you can get on interrogatories is quite simple: put all the information requested on a separate sheet of paper, answer everything as fully and as truthfully as you can, and then submit the materials to your attorney. Let your lawyer do the editing. Don't gloss over facts that you consider harmful (or even disastrous) to your case -- your lawyer must know everything, including the material that can prove detrimental to your case. Otherwise, how can you expect him or her to respond if the fact is disclosed in open court?

If, for instance, you are making a claim for an accident

you were involved in, you may feel reluctant to disclose the answer to a question in your interrogatories inquiring whether or not you've filed similar claims in the past. Perhaps you've been involved in a number of other cases in the past, and feel that revealing that information would damage your position.

Guess what? *Not* revealing that information -- at least to your own attorney -- could turn out to be a catastrophic mistake. The opposing lawyer need only check with a central claim reporting bureau -- to which most insurance companies have easy access -- and the case is, for all practical purposes, finished. You've failed to divulge specifically requested information on your interrogatory. You have a past history of pursuing what appear now to be morally questionable claims. Your lawyer may be good, but he or she probably isn't a magician. The jury won't need much time to reach a conclusion, and it won't be one you like.

On the other hand, if you've informed your lawyer about your background, he or she can take action to soften or dissipate the impact of the facts when they do arise. Let your lawyer decide what should or should not appear in the interrogatory. Remember that everything you disclose to him or her is privileged and cannot be divulged without your permission.

Frequently, interrogatories will contain questions that seem unfair, irrelevant, or burdened with needless detail. In the cases of questions that appear truly pointless, cruel, or diversionary, ask your attorney about the issue. He or she can help you provide an appropriate response. If your adversary finds this response unacceptable and persists, the court can review the matter at a later date. Remember that you have a right and responsibility -- particularly in highly technical or complex cases -- to make sure the lawyer asks the right questions in the interrogatory your side presents to the opposition. Virtually any lawyer can assemble a passable interrogatory if the suit involves an injury sustained due to a fall down an old, ill-maintained, and dangerous staircase; on the other hand, if the question concerns the professional conduct of a molecular biologist, and you have training in the field that your lawyer doesn't, you might want to discuss the interrogatory with him or her in some detail.

"DID I SAY THAT?"

What if you make a mistake? What if you answer a question incorrectly or respond inaccurately to a seemingly minor query that somehow takes on more importance in hindsight? If this occurs early enough in the process, the answer is a simple one: amend your response. Make every attempt to do so well before the trial begins. Interrogatories can, in most jurisdictions, be amended some weeks before the trial date. Once you step into the courtroom, however, it is very difficult to retract a false or inaccurate answer without seriously compromising your position.

A good attorney will not need to be reminded on the point, but you must always obtain a complete copy of all responses submitted to the court before you give any kind of testimony whatsoever. You must review these answers before you give a deposition or testify in court. If you contradict your interrogatory on the stand, you often won't hear about it from the opposing counsel until the point shows up in a powerful closing argument to the jury. Know what you said. Know what your case is. Review your case thoroughly.

LIVING THROUGH THE DEPOSITION

The deposition is your first real face-to-face encounter with the opposition lawyer, and, as such, it can be a little disconcerting. Nevertheless, with a calm approach and a concerted effort to work with your attorney, you can make sure your case is still presented in the best possible light.

As you may remember, a deposition (which usually takes place in the office of one of the attorneys) is sworn, out-of-court testimony given verbally by a litigant, lay witness, or expert witness. Everything said is recorded by a court stenographer who will prepare a transcript for later use. There are certain guidelines you should be familiar with before beginning the complex and frequently confusing ritual that is a deposition. Examine with care the points below before you sit down with your adversary for the first time.

Because you probably will not be questioned by your lawyer, you will depend on the opposition to state the "rules of the road" at the outset of your interview. Listen closely to the opening remarks the opposing attorney makes.

WHATEVER YOU DO, DON'T...

Don't answer any question you find difficult to understand. Ask the attorney to rephrase questions that seem too complex. If there is an unfamiliar or highly technical word or phrase contained in the question, ask that it be defined. It is counsel's responsibility to formulate clear questions.

Don't answer any question you haven't heard completely. Lawyers often change direction in mid-sentence. If you feel you haven't gotten the whole idea, don't answer. If you do, you well be harming your case.

Don't do the other attorney's work. If you volunteer information, submit to flattery, or even answer a question in such a way that opens new doors for the other side, you may as well invite the other side to sit in on your private conferences.

Don't forget to verbalize your responses. The people with you in the room may see you point to your injured left wrist, but unless somebody says something, it won't show up in the stenographer's transcript. If you forget to specify what you are pointing to or how you are repeating a gesture or motion, you may have difficulty convincing a jury that your courtroom testimony is consistent with your deposition.

Don't speak while someone else is speaking. Stenographers aren't magicians. If the court reporter has to choose between writing down what you say and what the opposing attorney says, the lawyer will win -- and you will lose. If the jury has to choose between what you say and what the court reporter wrote down, the court reporter will win -- and you will lose.

Don't guess. If you aren't sure of the answer to a question, say so. If you are sure, state the facts plainly. Once you guess, you can limit your attorney's future strategic options or, worse, impeach your own credibility. Even if it's only a matter of the way you phrase your responses, guessing makes you sound weak. If, at the time of the automobile accident that is the central issue in the case, you were going fifteen miles per hour, and you're asked during the deposition how fast you were going, what are you going to say? If you say "I was going fifteen miles an hour," you sound strong and self-assured. If you say "I think I was going somewhere around fifteen miles an hour, in that area, I imagine, but you know, it could have been five miles up or down in either direction; let's say fifteen," then you sound like a weak-kneed (and possibly deceptive) litigant.

Don't ignore objections. If your attorney objects to a question, stop your answer until he or she tells you whether you should continue. Depositions are often reduced to "fishing expeditions" -- in which lawyers ask seemingly irrelevant questions in the hope that those inquiries will lead to information valuable to their case. Some of the questions may be inappropriate. It is your attorney's duty to prevent you from answering questions that are improper in form or scope.

Your attorney may object to a question and then allow

you to answer it. By objecting, your lawyer is preserving his or her right to request that the court strike the question and response at a later date.

If your lawyer tells you to answer a question, do so. If you believe the answer should not be given, ask for a recess to discuss the question in private.

Finally, don't argue with the opposing lawyer. If he or she is snide, sarcastic, or rude, don't try to administer charm lessons. Your attorney is being paid to deal with the other side. If you let the opposing lawyer "get your goat," you may be participating in an experiment designed to make you demonstrate what it takes to get you to make foolish factual errors. Let your questioner rant and rave.

CHAPTER SEVEN
The Trial -- What You Must Do To Win

WHAT WILL WIN THE CASE?

Facts don't win cases. People do. The general impression left by the personalities involved in the conflict, the chemistry between an attorney and a jury or judge, even the physical appearance of a crucial witness -- these are the things that can win or lose legal conflicts.

Like it or not, in the battle between style and substance, style frequently takes the prize in the courtroom. In this chapter, we'll be looking at the ways you and your attorney can use this principle to your advantage as you wage your case in court.

APPEARANCE IS EVERYTHING

Particularly in jury trials, what you wear and how you present yourself is frequently just as important as what you say. And it starts being important well before you take the stand to testify.

Surprised? Don't be. Hours or days can pass between the time the jury is selected and the time you're scheduled to give testimony. During that period, you will be, in a very real sense, on trial whether you know it or not. Everyone forms first impressions based on appearance when they are introduced to someone: juries are no different.

While your attorney and the witnesses friendly to your case are arguing in your favor, you are making persuasive arguments of your own -- either attractive or unattractive -- simply by sitting and watching the proceedings. If you don't appear as the jury expects you to appear (and there are very real expectations to be addressed, even though they will never be stated outright) no testimony or argument will be as effective as you have a right to expect.

Once a jury has formed an initial impression, it's very difficult to reverse it. People are seldom enthusiastic about admitting -- even to themselves -- that their appraisals are incorrect. That's why it's your job to create a favorable impression from the very first instant you are seen by the jury -- or judge, for that matter.

How is this accomplished? There are some standard guidelines you should follow that will ensure that you are perceived in a positive light; they're outlined on the next page. Use these ideas as a starting point for discussions with your attorney on this subject.

For men: Avoid garish or loud clothing at all costs. Wear a sport shirt, a solid white or blue shirt, and a conservative tie. Do not wear excessive jewelry or open-collared shirts. If you are a businessman, "dress the part" by selecting the same suit you might wear to an important board meeting or presentation.

Your hair should be neat and not long; mustaches, too, are acceptable as long as they're well-groomed. Unless you are a professor, it isn't advisable to wear a beard.

Never wear glasses that change color -- in the courtroom, they will darken and give the distinct impression that you're trying to hide something. (It goes without saying that a litigant must -- unless he or she is legally blind -- stay away from standard dark sunglasses.)

For women: Again, be fairly conservative: don't wear flashy or avant-garde styles.

Use makeup judiciously. Avoid tight-fitting clothes. If you normally wear eyeglasses, wear them to the courtroom. You must see the person who will be cross-examining you.

If you're involved in a negligence case, it's probably a bad idea to select high heels when it comes to footwear. Imagine what the jurors will think in, say, a case in which you're suing for injuries sustained in a fall, if you stumble awkwardly from your seat, across the floor, and into the witness stand!

PROPER "ETIQUETTE" DURING JURY SELECTION, THE OPENING STATEMENT, AND EXAMINATION OF WITNESSES

In the early stages of the trial, your lawyer is attempting to establish a rapport with the jury. Your actions and body language must not hinder this process. (Remember that even though the jury has not been selected yet, it *is* sitting there among all the prospective jurors!)

You must appear attentive to questions and comments made by the lawyers and the judge. You must be careful to appear intelligent, at ease, and professional at all times -- and be certain, for instance, not to slouch in your seat or chew gum.

The opposing attorney will make statements you will consider unflattering, unfair, and inaccurate in the early going. That's to be expected. Don't glower or smirk at every offending phrase or mutter ominously beneath your breath. Juries -- and judges -- react very badly to such behavior, as it gives the impression you are vindictive and hot-tempered.

Never say anything out loud unless you are asked to do so. If you must speak to your attorney, turn towards him or her and say what you have to say at close quarters. *Don't* cup your hand over your mouth. You will appear to be concealing information -- because that's exactly what you'll be doing.

Establish a discreet method of informing your

attorney if (and why) there is a prospective juror you do not want to see selected. This way, your lawyer can determine whether your instincts are worth following. Whatever you do, though, *be discreet.* If the juror eventually is selected, you don't want his first impression of you and your case to be a tactless, overloud whisper questioning his or her suitability. (It's probably a good idea to establish realistic communication methods for use throughout the trial. You might agree with your attorney to write notes -- in very large and easily legible handwriting -- that he or she can read quickly without breaking a train of thought.)

When witnesses (friendly or unfriendly), testify, remain silent. Do not nod vehemently in agreement or shake your head solemnly at what you consider to be a misstatement.

A jury, by its very nature, functions as an independent body. If it senses that a litigant is trying to control testimony, it will overcompensate by attempting to maintain the objectivity it was instructed to bring to the case.

In short, it will discredit your witness or give undue credence to the witness you attempt -- even silently -- to contradict.

It is a natural reaction to smile at a witness who seems to have helped your cause, to wink, to murmur a word of thanks as he or she passes by. Don't do it. You can thank the witness later. Doing so in front of the jury will tarnish the witness's (and your) credibility. Accordingly, you should be sure that, if a personal friend is planning to testify for you, make certain that you instruct the person not to gesture or say anything to you as he or she enters and exits the courtroom.

In general, do everything you can to let your attorney do the job. Try not to interrupt the proceedings in any way: doing so will give the jury the impression that your case has not been well-prepared. A jury usually equates an unprepared lawyer with a meritless case.

ON THE STAND:
PERCEPTIONS AND FACTS

In this area, it's a good idea to review the basic principle that underlies everything in the case from your wardrobe selection to your laywer's presentation to the judge or jury. That principle is a simple one, and it is, one hopes, a familiar one as well by this point: *appearance is everything.* As you might expect, the idea holds true when the subject is that of witnesses, as well.

What may seem to you to be a less-than-crucial piece of information can take on undue significance because of its expert delivery or the attractive personality of the other side's witness. That's the way things happen in court.

Conversely, you should be prepared for the possiblity that one of your witnesses may present a telling fact in an awkward, incoherent, or even offensive way. If that happens, and an important point's impact is minimized, it doesn't mean that the trial is rigged, that the other side is cheating, or that the judge is out to get you. It means your case is exactly like many, many others.

Don't let such events ruffle you or affect your composure. Remember that the jury may be watching *you* at any given moment. Stay as relaxed and calmly attentive as possible.

COMPETENCY

In most state and federal courts, a witness is assumed to be competent to testify until proven otherwise. What *is* competency? Broadly speaking, a witness must be able to express him or herself (directly or through an interpreter), must understand the duty to tell the truth, and must have personal knowledge of the matter in question.

If an objection is made by your adversary's attorney as to your witness's competency, the first step the court will take is to examine the witness while the jury is not in presence. If the judge agrees that the witness lacks competency, the jury will not hear that witness. This does not happen often. Obviously, it will not help your case to have the jury see your witness step up to the stand, only to be challenged successfully and never heard from again! (This, too, is a fairly rare occurrence; the most likely scenario is one in which your lawyer anticipates the problem and asks your opponent if he or she intends to challenge the witness's right to testify.)

Some surprising facts accompany this issue. For example, there is no fixed age at which children are excluded from testifying; an extremely young child who meets the guidelines may give less than reliable testimony, but that does not prevent the jury from hearing it. A mentally disabled person can testify as well -- as long as he or she understands the nature of the oath taken, and is able to communicate relevant facts. Again, such testimony may not be the most "solid" supplied over the course of the trial, but there's no reason the jury can't take it into account.

There are a number of possible reasons behind a judge's decision not to allow a witness to testify. He or she might find that the testimony given would be misleading, tend to confuse, or simply present a basic disability of testimonial qualities.

These instances, however, are quite rare. You and your attorney, therefore, should assume that, leaving aside privileged individuals, your opponent's witnesses will in all likelihood end up testifying, regardless of their age, bias, and perspective on the case.

PRIVILEGE

Your attorney cannot call just anyone as a witness, or ask anything he or she wants of the witnesses that are called. The law has, over the years, erected certain privileges which prohibit various types of testimony. Such privileges pertain to confidential communications made between certain groups or classes of people. While the standards from state to state will vary as to the number of recognized privileges, the underlying premises are always the same: trust and confidentiality. *Keep in mind that specifics will vary;* not all states will institute the same guidelines. If you are in *any* doubt about whether or not your communications with an individual is privileged, consult an attorney for the standards in your state.

Here are some of the main classes of privilege accorded by a number of states that allow exemption from testifying in a case.

Attorney-client privilege. This is the most common form. As we learned earlier, whatever you tell your lawyer is privileged, as long as the communication was made during the attorney-client relationship with no one else present. Your side cannot cross-examine your adversary about what he or she said about the case to counsel.

There are limitations on the privilege. If you were to speak with your lawyer about future criminal intentions -- inform him or her that you planned to rob a bank, for instance -- that information would not be protected. In addition, if you later sue your attorney for any reason, he or she may testify against you regarding the facts and conversations that related to the subject of the lawsuit. And if the police were to ask your attorney whether or not he saw bloodstains on your clothing at your first meeting, your attorney would not be able to claim attorney-client privilege and refuse to answer: observations are not covered under the privilege, though a conversation about your bloodstained clothing would be.

Husband-wife privilege. Confidential communications between spouses are privileged. Check with your lawyer regarding the standards that apply in your state. You can encounter some limitations on this privilege. If you are asked about communications between you and your spouse that were not confidential -- words that could be shown, for example, to have been spoken loudly in the presence of some third party -- that conversation would not be privileged, and could be legitimately be exposed by an opposing attorney.

As with the attorney-client privilege, this series of protections applies only to communications, and not, for instance, to lawful searches.

Physician-patient privilege. Usually, any communications you make to your doctor or dentist which relate to your medical treatment are privileged. Similar standards may pertain to communications with a psychologist, psychiatrist, or other therapist. Consult with your attorney for the applicable local guidelines.

WITNESSES: LAY AND EXPERT

"Your" witnesses cannot testify about every element in the case. Neither can "theirs." There are different kinds of witnesses, each used to establish a certain set of facts. Some of the facts you feel need to be established may not, in the long run, be as relevant to the court as they are to you.

Let's begin at the beginning and examine the first major distinguishing factors that arise in any discussion of witnesses.

Courts draw a distinction between lay witnesses and expert witnesses. A lay witness is one who does not necessarily have any special skills in a given field, but is, as a result of involvement with the issues of the case, in a position to testify about his or her direct sensory exposure to the conflict. Not what he or she feels, thinks, or believes ought to have happened, or did happen under similar circumstances some time ago, or heard happened from someone else. All that's open to discussion is what took place in his or her own experience: more specifically, what was seen, heard, smelled, touched, or tasted -- and nothing else. A businessman testifying in an arson case, for instance, can testify that he saw the fire; that he heard the fire engines, that he smelled smoke in the air. He cannot, however, testify as to the cause of the blaze unless he qualifies as an expert witness.

How would he do that? What is an expert witness?

An expert witness is one who, by virtue of knowledge, skill, training, education, or experience in some specialized area, possesses information not generally known by the layman. An expert is permitted to offer an opinion as to the cause of a particular event. An expert's testimony is allowed to function as an aid to those determining the outcome of the case in penetrating to the heart of an event or condition they normally would not encounter. In short, the expert is considered to have more data to rely upon in giving testimony than a lay witness. The lay witness is familiar with the event itself; the expert witness can gain some (admittedly second-hand) exposure to an event, and also bring to bear his or her specialized training or experience.

Before a witness can testify as an expert, he or she must be qualified by the court. This procedure is usually performed while the jury is not present, and involves examination and cross-examination of the witness on the topics of his or her education, training, and experience. The field of expertise or professional discipline in question often is examined in detail so the court can determine whether or not a "borderline" field of study has attained general scientific or educational acceptance. If, after this, the court determines that the witness is an expert, he or she may testify.

The fact that the court permits a witness to testify does not constitute an endorsement of the opinions that will be given in court. Generally, the jury has a great deal of discretion in deciding how much weight should be attributed to an expert's testimony. It's possible that a jury might decide to accept the expert's word on the matter confidently; adopt some portions of the testimony as valid and discard other portions; or disregard the expert's views altogether. While an expert's testimony cannot dictate how a case must be decided, it can enhance important points.

Keep in mind that expert witnesses can be located in virtually any field of endeavor, and can end up on either end of an argument -- depending on who's paying the bills. If one expert says that an industrial accident was caused by "X", another expert will appear who declares that it was actually precipitated by an abundance of "Y". If for some reason an expert can't realistically claim "Y" as the main cause, you can expect a persuasive argument to the effect that the presence of excess "X" is completely irrelevant and has no bearing on the events.

Whoever said "talk is cheap" probably never had to arrange for a doctor, scientist, or engineer to testify in court. Expert witness talk can be quite pricey, and frequently cancels itself out when the other side can afford as much as you can. When your attorney tells you he or she has engaged an expert witness to help solidify your position, don't expect your opponent to capitulate immediately out of stark terror at the prospect of confronting someone who Knows What's What. Experts are a permanent feature of the legal landscape. It's a pretty good bet your expert already has been seen in action by the opposing attorney, and offers far less in the way of competitive advantage than you think!

CHARACTER, PAST ACTIONS, AND YOUR WITNESSES

You may be tempted to instruct your lawyer to call all your friends and business associates and use them as witnesses against your adversary. They know what kind of person you're dealing with! They can testify that your opponent is an unscrupulous, evil-minded opportunist, who has a past history of problems just like this!

Tempting though it may be, it is almost always a waste of time to attempt to introduce such testimony. Unless your friends can introduce specific facts based on their own experiences *in this particular conflict*, it's a good bet that you can't introduce the testimony.

Evidence of a person's character traits -- positive or negative -- are not admissible to prove that he or she acted in conformity with those traits. The fact that fifty of your friends are prepared to swear that your adversary is, in general, a nasty and unprincipled individual is irrelevant. The testimony would not prove that any specific actions took place, proper or improper. (Of course, if your lawyer is trying to establish that a person has a reputation as an untruthful person whose testimony should be viewed with suspicion, then relevant past actions and statements take on greater importance.)

Even if your adversary has been *convicted* of a similar crime or lost an *identical* case, you should not expect those facts to be the central elements of your lawyer's arguments. Evidence that a person committed a crime or negligent act in the past is not evidence that he or she committed the present crime or careless act.

OFF LIMITS

There are other areas which your attorney cannot highlight in the testimony that accompanies your case, much as you might wish to see them explored for all to see. Here's a rundown of some areas clients frequently suggest that witnesses bring up in testimony, but which are, alas, often off limits. Here as elsewhere, specifics will differ from state to state.

Remedial conduct. In many states, you cannot

attempt to prove your case by introducing evidence of your adversary's efforts to remedy a potential area of negligence or wrongdoing after the fact. Let's suppose you're walking through a drugstore one day when you catch your heel in a hole in the floor, fall, and break your wrist. You decide to sue. Several weeks later, a friend of yours walks past the store and notices through the front window that an employee is patching the hole. In a number of states, your friend cannot testify that the storeowner's instructions to repair the hole constitute negligence in your fall.

Offers of compromise. Your opponent may have offered to settle your dispute. If, for whatever reason, that offer was not accepted (or if it was withdrawn), that evidence is inadmissible. The legal system encourages compromise, and as a result, will not permit testimony regarding settlement overtures, successful or unsuccessful. If every offer to settle a trial constituted an admission of wrongdoing -- and to a jury, that's almost certainly the impression that would be left -- no incentive would exist to settle any case! You may feel that your adversary's offer "proves" that you're "right," but you'd better not let the jury in on your opinion. If you blurt out anything about the offer, you'll probably watch helplessly as the court directs a mistrial, forcing you to retry your case. Think about it: that sounds like a time-consuming, expensive, and very unpleasant possibility, doesn't it? It is.

Liability insurance and offers to pay medical expenses. No witness can introduce the fact that insurance or any other payment plan exists to cover any award in the case. The presence or absence of insurance (or any similar post-verdict financial arrangement) has nothing whatsoever to do with the merits of a case, and cannot be brought to the attention of the jury.

YOUR DIRECT EXAMINATION

Finally! Your turn to tell your side!

"Telling" is an appropriate word, for your testimony really should be the recounting of a story. Everyone likes a good story -- one with a beginning, middle, and end, and a clear point. Juries are no different.

A jury *wants* to hear a clear, logical narration of the events in question. The simpler the story, the more likely it will be accepted. The clearer the characters, the more persuasive its delineation of right and wrong.

Before you testify, you will, no doubt, review your "story" several times with your lawyer. There are several reasons for this. First of all, your lawyer wants to prepare you for the questions he or she will ask you. While it is possible for the opposing attorney's questions (which will come a little later on) to take you by surprise, there's no excuse for this happening while your attorney is in charge.

In addition, your lawyer will want to make sure you're accustomed to the stilted phraseology that will be employed in court. It is an unfortunate fact that courtroom questions frequently bear no resemblance to standard, conversational English.

Finally, a good attorney will review your testimony to ease any nervousness you may feel about taking the stand. Many people put speaking in public at or near the top of their list of most frightening experiences. If addressing a Rotary or Kiwanis meeting gives you the willies, it's a good bet that addressing a jury, judge, or perhaps even a packed courtroom will bring on a good degree of apprehension as well. As we've learned, however, appearance is everything in court, and the appearance of relaxation and openness is important to project. Once you're familiar with the sequence and substance of the questions posed, and can respond lucidly and intelligently to them, it will be your lawyer's duty to see that the story flows smoothly and coherently.

There are, however, many techniques that you can, and must, employ to assist your attorney. Let's examine what these techniques are, and in what environment you can expect to use them.

The first thing to take into account about the environment is that, in the vast majority of cases, the jury *wants you to succeed.* It is a rare juror indeed who wants to see someone embarrassed on the stand. Each juror was on stage during the selection process. Each was probably as uneasy about the ordeal as you will be. You can count on receiving a certain amount of sympathy as you recount your story.

It's also important to remember that you are not alone -- at least not at this stage. (Things can seem pretty one-sided once you're subjected to cross-examination.) Even though your lawyer is not the one in the spotlight, he or she is very much your partner in the direct examination, and can be counted upon to guide you through the process. Don't worry about forgetting to say "the right thing." Your attorney, by now, should know your case inside and out. If you forget to mention an important fact, he or she will direct the questioning in such a way as to allow you to address it.

You can see why it is *vitally* important that you listen carefully to your attorney during your direct examination. Don't raise issues that aren't contained in the question you're asked; don't repeat yourself; just answer the question clearly and succinctly, then stop talking.

When you respond to a question, answer in a clear, loud voice. Not only must your lawyer hear the response -- it's imperative that the jury and the judge hear every word, too. Many people have a habit of allowing their voices to trail off at the end of a sentence. This may be fine in casual conversation, but deadly in a courtroom setting. Overcompensate by making a conscious effort to speak in the same tone until you have finished your answer -- even if it feels slightly uncomfortable. Imagine that you are speaking for the benefit of a relative who's slightly hard of hearing, and seated behind the table at which your lawyer usually sits. Project your voice. This way the jury will be sure to hear everything you say.

It's important, unless otherwise instructed, to direct your comments to your attorney, and not to the jury. If you simply maintain eye contact with your lawyer throughout your direct examination, you will project an image that's confident, honest, and straightforward. An experienced attorney will change his position throughout your testimony, being sure to wind up near the jury at key points of the narrative. This will ensure that you actually will be facing the jury, naturally, when you highlight the important parts of your story.

Keep your wording simple. If you are an expert in a field that requires the use of complex or technical terminology, respond in the most direct way you can and immediately explain any phrases that may be unfamiliar to a judge or jury. Don't expect a jury to guess. They usually will either guess wrong or wait for opposing counsel to explain the matter to them.

Be careful not to project an image that is either too haughty or too submissive. State your facts with confidence and respect for all parties. Do not crack jokes. If levity is required, your lawyer will provide it.

Avoid characterizing your opponent in any way, unless you are asked specifically by your counsel to do so. If you are asked about your opponent, *don't use questionable language in court.* You may consider your opponent to be an S.O.B., but selecting a more diplomatic response will heighten your standing.

If an objection is posed by the opposing attorney, stop talking immediately. The judge must rule on the objection, and will not want to do battle with you over who has the floor. If you continue speaking, you may receive a judicial reprimand.

The judge will rule on each objection, identifying it as either *sustained* or *overruled.* If the objection is sustained you cannot finish your response. Never argue with a judge over a ruling on an objection -- or on anything, for that matter. There is simply no advantage whatsoever in doing so. Cross a judge in front of a jury, and you alienate not only the judge but also the jury.

If the judge asks you a question (usually to clarify an ambiguous point in your testimony), turn and answer politely, being sure to insert the phrase "Your Honor" in your response. Remember that the jury is watching your interplay with the primary authority figure involved in the case. Don't equivocate or attempt any sarcasm whatsoever. Even if the answer is painful, provide it to the judge. A single damaging, but truthful, response often won't lose a case. An intentionally evasive or deceptive one may.

If your attorney interrupts you, there's a reason. He or she probably is attempting to focus your response on a particular area. Listen to the question posed after the interruption, and respond calmly and confidently. *Let your attorney lead the testimony.*

When you are handed an exhibit to review on the witness stand, look at it closely. If it is a document, read it -- don't just glance at it. Take the time to examine the exhibit before answering in any way. (Of course, before you testify, you should visit the scenes of any accidents, review all pertinent documents, review your interrogatory and deposition testimony, and inspect all proposed exhibits in the company of your attorney.)

Face your attorney when testifying concerning an exhibit -- don't stare down at the object, as this will cause problems for others in hearing your response.

As you did in your deposition, speak affirmatively, avoiding such phrases as "I guess" and "I believe." If you make a mistake in your response, correct it quickly. Remember that it is far more damaging for your opponent's lawyer to uncover your slip than it is for you to admit the error during your direct examination.

If your lawyer asks you to describe something, do so thoroughly and completely. Don't assume the judge or jury will understand what you're talking about. They won't. They have not lived with the case for as many months as you have. Provide all relevant details and background information.

If you're asked to draw a diagram, *make it big.* The jury will be sitting some distance away from you. Make sure the ideas you want to get across are easily discernable. Don't describe the diagram until you have completed drawing it. Remember that no one expects you to provide fully realized architectural renderings. What will be expected is that you be able to describe what you have drawn.

If someone enters the courtroom during your testimony, pause until the individual is seated and you can continue without distraction. This will allow both you and the jury to regain composure and attention to the issue at hand.

If you normally use hand gestures when you speak, do so on the witness stand. Try to make yourself as comfortable as possible while testifying. If you feel stilted, your speech and demeanor will appear stilted. While it will probably be somewhat difficult to relax, make every attempt to do so. The more relaxed you are, the more natural and believable your testimony will be.

Stay away from analogies and anecdotes that don't relate directly to the case. You'll probably notice that lawyers use them quite often to illustrate key points and make complex concepts accessible. Awkward or misapplied comparisons, however, can backfire, and give your opposition a powerful weapon to use against you.

You may be tempted to use some of the objects in your immediate surroundings to illustrate a point that requires some sort of visual presentation. If you must do so, use a nearby pad of paper, a briefcase, or a box of index cards; but whatever you do, *never use the Bible on which you took your oath.* This is one of the seemingly unimportant details that can make a difference in how your case is viewed by the jury.

Finally, and perhaps most importantly, *do not worry about how the judge or jury is reacting to your testimony.* Handling such perceptions is your lawyer's job; furthermore, beyond presenting your testimony in as persuasive and straightforward a manner as possible, you have no control over "how the show is playing." Don't try to decipher anything until you have the chance to discuss your case in private with your attorney. Until then, just let the facts speak for themselves and let your attorney do the work.

THE HEAT IS ON:
CROSS-EXAMINATION

Eventually, of course, you will have to face the opposing side's attorney. What will you do?

To reduce the answer to its simplest dimensions, you should do exactly what you did under direct examination, when your attorney was in charge. Relax, be yourself, state the facts as you know them, and don't volunteer anything that isn't asked for.

Forty years of television courtroom dramas have taught most litigants to dread what they consider to be the high point of the legal conflict: the chance the opposing attorney has to tear them to shreds, unmask them, put all their faults under a spotlight. What usually happens is that a litigant is so terrified at the prospect of confronting Perry Mason that the real-life opposing attorney has very little difficulty making all the points on his or her agenda -- without resorting to any melodramatic techniques at all.

Think about it. If you're so frightened of the mere prospect of cross-examination that you unknowingly alter your appearance, aren't you doing the other side's work? Your opposition wants to see you rigid, tense, ill-spoken, hostile, and evasive. They want to hear answers that are tentative and apparently intended to deceive. They want you to appear ill at ease, uncertain of your case, and likely to mislead the court if given the opportunity.

And that's exactly how you'll look if you feel you must brace yourself for an onslaught that may or may not materialize! It's a far wiser course to remain as calm as possible, answer the questions, and stick with the facts you know.

Different lawyers will adopt different strategies in the cross-examination. Some may seek to antagonize you. Some may attempt to "kill you with kindness." Some may do their best to confuse and disorient you. But whatever the approach, the objective always remains the same: discredit you by taking advantage of some weakness in your personality or a fact you are unprepared to confront. If you're not relaxed, that job becomes much easier. Regardless of the approach the opposing attorney takes, you must view what he or she does during cross-examination objectively. Your lawyer has a job to do; so does the lawyer for the other side. In most instances, cross-examination won't consist of attacks upon you personally, but rather upon the facts you present. *This is an important distinction.*

Try to ignore the tone the opposing attorney takes; focus instead on the question. Give the question the fullest, most confident answer you can. Be forceful, but not defensive. Don't let the cross-examiner divert you from your real purpose: responding to the query with an accurate answer.

Don't try to outguess your cross-examiner. Don't assume that every question has an ulterior motive, or will, if answered openly, inevitably lead to a sequence of questions designed to embarrass you. If you spend your time attempting to anticipate the questions the opposing attorney may ask next, you will diminish your testimony's effectiveness.

Is there *anything* you can do besides sit there and take it? In a broad sense, yes. You can have a good idea of the techniques most lawyers use during cross-examination -- but you should not let that knowledge fool you into thinking you can compete on an equal basis with the opposing attorney. Your purpose is not to compete. Your purpose is to project a confident, open, honest image as you answer questions.

That having been said, let's examine the most

common methods used by attorneys to gain an advantage during cross-examination.

One potent weapon is the leading question. A lawyer may ask you a question that's phrased in such a way as to allow only a yes-or-no response. As you might guess, there's not much likelihood of either response making you look great in the eyes of the judge or jury.

If you cannot answer the question as posed -- if the topic at issue cannot be reduced to a yes-or-no response -- you must say so tactfully, and explain without delay why you cannot answer the question in that manner. If you fail to explain this in short order, the judge will probably direct you to answer the question. Of course, you may be directed to respond even after you've explained matters; in that case, you have no alternative but to answer, even if you consider the response less than complete or harmful to your case. Your lawyer will have the opportunity to shed some light on the problem when he or she conducts your redirect examination, which occurs after your opponent's cross-examination.

Another technique frequently used by cross-examining attorneys is to state a series of apparently innocuous facts and ask for your agreement on their validity. Once you reach the fourth or fifth fact, the lawyer hopes, you will have been convinced that there's no danger in assenting to anything that hops out of his or her mouth. That's when things get interesting. Suddenly you're agreeing to facts that are in dispute, facts you are unfamiliar with, or facts that aren't facts at all.

The best way to deal with this approach is, quite simply, not to agree with your adversary for the sake of agreement. Hold your ground. If you are not sure whether or not something is true, *say that you don't know*. Remember, you were involved in the incident(s) at the heart of the case; the attorneys, the jury, and the judge were not. No one knows the facts more fully than you. If you stick forcefully to your story and don't get sidetracked, there is nothing the cross-examiner can do. He or she may mock your testimony or attempt to cast aspersions on your reliability, but there's really not as much room for this sort of thing as you may imagine. In real-life courtrooms, which are very different from the television variety, argumentative questions are usually looked upon with disfavor. Most judges will direct an attorney overusing such questions to stop once your attorney has made an objection.

Another method employed to disorient you during cross-examination does take advantage of television-style dramatic flair. The key to it lies in the opposing attorney's desire to see you contradict yourself rather than admit a mistake. Here's how it might work. The cross-examiner reads from your earlier deposition testimony or from your interrogatory answers, and in so doing highlights an area of the record that conflicts with your present trial testimony. The cross-examiner then inquires whether your present recollection of the event is better than it was at the time that you answered interrogatories or submitted to a deposition.

Unless there is a reason to consider your present version better, your best bet is to go back to the earlier version of events. The jury will assume that the event was freshest in your mind at that time. Admit to the cross-examiner that the earlier testimony or document refreshes your recollection and corrects a mistake in your testimony. (On the other hand, if a rational explanation *does* exist for the discrepancy, explain it.)

Make certain that you look at the cross-examiner when you deliver your answer. *Never* look to your attorney for assistance. An urgent look directed to you attorney will convey the impression that you're trapped, that your story is unraveling. That's not the image that you want to project -- particularly if the issue is an unimportant one. There's a pretty fair likelihood that the issue is a minor one, intended solely to discredit you, and having little direct bearing on the case.

You are human. You will not be expected to provide photographic recall on every query, particularly if the opposing attorney is inquiring after minute and irrelevant facts in an obvious effort to discredit your capacity to remember details. Try not to get flustered. If you don't remember something, admit it.

Rational people realize that you don't enter into a contract on the assumption that it will not be fulfilled; people know that no one steps into an automobile with the objective of remembering any event that may take place during an accident. Be yourself. Stick with the version of events you have established with your lawyer. Stay calm.

NO ONE HAS
A PERFECT CASE

In preparing you for cross-examination, your attorney will go over the weakest points of your case, as these are the ones that you're likely to hear most about on the stand. *Every* case has such weak points. Don't expect to win on every issue. Even though your cross-examiner may try to badger and intimidate you, retain your composure. (Remember that jurors often side with the underdog!) As long as you are forthright and pleasant in your responses, you will have achieved your purpose.

SUMMATION:
WHAT TO EXPECT

Unpleasant things are said during summation -- the point in the trial where the lawyers tie up their arguments into a single package and make their most passionate pleas for their version of events.

It's a good idea to be prepared for some "hardballs" to be thrown your way during this portion of the trial. Your character, actions, and memory will be assailed. If there were no reason for such verbal attacks to take place, there would be no lawsuit. Most people are unaccustomed to being criticized openly and in great detail. Take such criticism, put it in open court, and you may have a hard pill indeed to swallow.

As difficult as it may be, however, you must remain stoic during the summation period. The jury will be watching you intently to gauge your reactions to the charges leveled against you. A sudden outburst or unpleasant facial expression may reinforce your opponent's version of the case's facts. You've made it this far; don't destroy your work and the work of your attorney by mumbling, shifting uneasily, or appearing to challenge the opposing attorney. Sit still, stare straight ahead, and don't react in any way whatsoever.

CHAPTER EIGHT: Jury Duty -- What They Say They Want You to Think, What They <u>Really</u> Want You to Think, and How to Tell Whether Or Not You Actually Think So

JURY DUTY: PEOPLE IN SUITS
TRYING TO CONVINCE YOU OF THINGS

There's a decent chance that, at some point in your life, you'll be called for jury duty. As we learned earlier, the process begins with a group of prospective jurors undergoing an evaluation from the opposing lawyers. Whether *you* are selected -- and what you will end up evaluating if you are -- are crucial issues to all parties, but of particular importance to the attorneys.

From the minute you enter the courtroom until the final seconds before you determine your verdict, the lawyers involved in the case will be (they hope) both inside and outside of your head, molding your perceptions, shaping the decisions you'll make, fashioning the simplest and most convincing version of the events in question. Whole treatises have been written on the art of courtroom presentation; careers rise and fall with the positive and negative responses a lawyer elicits from a jury.

What follows in this chapter is not meant to be an exhaustive compilation of all the "tricks of the trade," but rather an introduction to the complex and often bewildering world of strategy that accompanies any trial by jury. If you review the information that follows, you'll be in a better position to determine your true reaction to the facts of the case you'll be hearing.

Of course, even if you aren't selected for jury duty, but do plan on taking part in a court case that will be *decided* by a jury, it's a good idea to have an idea of what's going on during the selection process -- and beyond -- so you can plan your strategy effectively with your attorney.

WHY AND HOW JURORS ARE DISMISSED

Let's face it. Most people don't jump for joy the second they learn they've been selected for jury duty. If your primary objective is to be removed from consideration so as to avoid an inconvenient absence from work or other activities, read on. In this section we'll examine who wants which kind of juror -- and why -- as well as outlining the types of people usually dismissed during the preliminary stages.

As a prospective juror, you'll hear, in all probability, a brief message from the judge informing you that the intention of all involved, including the lawyers, is to work together to pick an impartial jury.

This is nonsense.

No competent attorney wants an impartial jury. During the initial stages, which, as we learned earlier, are known as the voir dire, each lawyer strives to win jurors that he or she considers favorable to the cause that must be argued. Lawyers will settle for a neutral jury but virtually never attempt to seat one.

If the lawyers (as opposed to the judge) are doing the questioning, the process is quite detailed and intricate. Depending upon the facts that underlie the case, attorneys can be expected to pose questions that are of greater or lesser sneakiness.

Is "sneaky" really the word? Yes. The objective is usually to unmask the juror's real feelings toward a particular subject or person, and either remove the juror from consideration or get him or her to lean toward a favorable position in the early stages. If the lawyer is successful in achieving the second goal, a late reversal during deliberation -- when the verdict is on the line -- will not be possible without loss of face in front of the other jurors.

In addition, a lawyer may attempt to identify himself and his client with a given juror during questioning, a more subtle technique calling on a certain degree of personal interplay. If the identification is successful, and the juror comes away with a *conscious or unconscious* conviction that the lawyer's client is "just like me," the juror is more likely to favor that client. (And one or two such jurors may hold the balance: a civil case requires an alignment of five-sixths of the jury on one side, and a criminal matter requires only one dissenting vote to "hang the jury.")

In both civil and criminal cases, each attorney is allowed a certain number of peremptory challenges -- that is, each lawyer can refuse a certain number of jurors for any reason he or she likes. If those challenges have all been used, other unacceptable jurors can be excused "for cause" -- which means that the judge must agree that there is a specific reason to excuse the juror from the case.

In civil cases, both sides have the same number of peremptory challenges. In criminal cases, however, defendants may have more peremptory challenges than the prosecution (this will vary from state to state). The prospective jurors usuallly do not know that each side has a limited number of peremptory challenges -- for all they know, the lawyers could continue striking jurors from the list forever. The judge however, as well as the opposing counsel, keep careful records of how many jurors have been stricken by an attorney.

Once one side has expended all of its peremptory challenges, the judge may call both attorneys to the bench and indicate, out of the jury's range of hearing, that one of the sides has reached its limit. Opposing counsel, of course, is free to continue issuing peremptory challenges until all that are allotted are similarly exhausted.

IF THE JUDGE IS IN CHARGE

If the court conducts the voir dire, the lawyers must work a little harder. Because the attorneys do not have the opportunity to question the jurors, they must make certain judgment calls about the way certain classes of people react to certain cases. They must also rely, to a large degree, on a combination of instinct and past experience to determine which jurors will be sympathetic to their cases.

What happens, in essence, is that the attorneys "pigeonhole" each prospective juror by weighing such factors as age, sex, occupation, and nationality. They also may consider numerous subtle clues, both verbal and non-verbal, that a juror may provide. The ultimate aim, of course, is to identify the jurors that fall into a category that can be considered to be favorable to the lawyer's cause -- or at least not hostile to it.

Every case is different. Every juror is different. Nevertheless, certain broad standards apply -- and are followed -- in the selection of jurors for various types of cases. It is true that, in doing all of this, there is a great deal of generality, assumption, and stereotyping. When no questions are permitted, however, there is no alternative.

Let's take a look at some of the factors taken into account during a court-conducted voir dire, and, to some extent, any jury selection process.

Age. The assumption made by most attorneys is that young adults are less likely to have fixed opinions, and may be more willing to accept new ideas or novel arguments, while older jurors often have preconceived notions and are unlikely to retreat from them. Unique fact patterns of the kind often advanced by plaintiffs in civil cases and defendants in criminal cases may, quite simply, not sell to an older jury.

The older juror is also considered less likely to return a high verdict in a comparatively insubstantial case. An individual well along in years and on a limited budget may pride him or herself on a knowledge of the "value of a dollar," and think twice before returning a dramatic award in a case in which the plaintiff is not injured seriously by the defendant.

Sex. In both civil and criminal cases, women are regarded as being skeptical of the testimony of other women.

An attorney will try to minimize the number of

women on the jury if a female client exhibits some character trait that might be considered damaging by female
jurors. Furthermore, if the client is an attractive young
woman, the tendency will be to gather as many men as
possible into the jury, on the assumption that men are
likely to identify with her and overlook any shortcomings
in the case more readily than they would with another litigant.

Occupation. Attorneys often attempt to gauge a
juror's prejudices or predispositions by the occupation
the person holds. Those affiliated with the arts, education, or social sciences usually are favored by attorneys
representing plaintiffs and criminal defendants, on the
assumption that such people will be more compassionate
and allow their feelings or convictions to overrule logic or
reason. Conversely, prosecutors and defense lawyers in
civil cases will choose managers and professionals, such
as bankers, engineers, and accountants, whom they consider to be less likely to be influenced by pleas for mercy
or money, because of a supposed reliance on precision
and deduction. Furthermore, upper- and middle-level
managers are considered to be less sympathetic to arguments that a business or corporation acted in an unreasonable manner.

Skilled craftsmen and self-employed businesspeople
are considered to hold wary attitudes toward injured
plaintiffs or criminal defendants. Some individuals with
an extensive work history are often assumed to exhibit a
strong work ethic and no inclinations toward lenient
verdicts or generous awards unless obviously "earned"
by the litigant. The self-employed businessperson

is probably accustomed to a position of power, used to having his or her opinions treated with respect, and assumed to think twice before allowing sympathy alone to influence a decision.

If your occupation is similar to that of an important party in the trial, you can expect to be rejected as a juror. You probably will be challenged in very short order for one of two reasons: either an attorney will presume that you'll identify too much with the individual in question, or you'll be considered too knowledgeable about an important aspect of the case, with the attendant risk that you may act as an (unpredictable) expert witness during the jury's deliberations. Lawyers like to be in control of their cases, and someone in possession of more facts than are at their disposal is considered dangerous.

THREE "TYPES" LAWYERS
HATE TO SEE ON THE JURY

If you're curious about the types of jurors likely to be dismissed from hearing your case on grounds of personality or bearing, or if you wish to project certain qualities that will help you attain your goal of dismissal, here are a number of profiles you may wish to review. Displaying signs from one or more of these categories is a good way for a juror to fail "the first cut."

The "life of the party." An indecisive, submissive type will score points with a plaintiff's lawyer or the defense in criminal case on the grounds that such a person will be extremely concerned about a wrongful conviction or uncompensated victim. On the other hand, an aggressive, loud, and perhaps genuinely humorous person will make both sides nervous. The "comedian" will be concerned, the theory goes, with his or her personal position in the jury's hierarchy -- and not with the case. Unlikely as it may seem, lawyers worry that he or she may even compete for attention with the litigants, attorneys, or even the judge at some point in the trial! Such a juror is considered a dangerously destabilizing element and usually will be dismissed rapidly.

The inattentive or hard-of-bearing. Trusting your case to someone whose occupation or nationality might seem attractive is one thing. But no sane lawyer will allow a person with an extremely short attention span, an inability to remember simple details, or a hearing disorder to sit on the jury -- no matter what he or she looks like or does for a living. Attempting to make a case in front of a person who either cannot understand you or will not remember your remarks the next day is roughly comparable to giving the juror a special coin with "guilty" imprinted on one side and "not guilty" on the other. Heads you win, tails you lose. That's not why lawyers spend all that time in law school.

The indecipherable. Prospective jurors who consistently give unconvincing, enigmatic, or seemingly dishonest replies to straightforward questions are looked upon with uneasiness. Failure to make eye contact, incomprehensible responses, half-finished or inappropriate remarks -- all of these are signals to a competent lawyer (or judge, for that matter) that the juror will, if selected, either lack the social skills necessary to work with a group, or bring some perspective to the case not in consonance with normal logic or reasoning. Unless either or both of the lawyers have exhausted their challenges, and the judge is more or less incompetent, such a juror will not be seated.

WHO'S WHO

There are exceptions to every rule and every generality, but in outlining and clarifying what a juror is likely to expect, some generalities are probably in order. For our purposes, a two-part breakdown is most effective in describing the two sides that will appeal to the jury's collective mind, emotions, and sense of justice. While there are thousands, perhaps hundreds of thousands, of different ways legal conflicts can arise in court, two main types of legal argument can serve to describe the atmosphere and dynamics that accompany a great many of the cases argued before juries. Let's examine them here.

The "little guy's" side. A lawyer defending a person accused of a crime, as well as one representing a plaintiff in, say, a personal injury case or a malpractice dispute, will tend to highlight the difficulties of an individual confronting "the system." Broadly speaking, "the system" can be our society's criminal justice mechanism, the medical or legal establishment, the monolithic stereotype associated with a large corporation or bureaucracy, or any of a dozen other institutions.

The "big guy's" side. Attorneys who argue the cases of businesses sued for negligence, doctors and lawyers sued for malpractice, or other groups or individuals accused by a plaintiff of wrongdoing -- as well as prosecutors in criminal cases -- tend to emphasize the recklessness, inconsistency, or even criminality of the individual or individuals at the center of the opposition's case. These lawyers must downplay claims of victimization, abuse, or complete innocence that issue from the other side. In the case of the criminal prosecutor, the titles of "the State" or "the People" may be appealed to in order to lend a sense of authority, public support, and legitimacy to the arguments put forward.

To be sure, there are legal conflicts that arise in which the "little guy-big guy" dichotomy is less obvious -- or perhaps even altogether irrelevant. But the models outlined above will provide a good a basis to evaluate the various directions in which a juror will be tugged during a trial.

WHAT THE "LITTLE GUY'S" SIDE MIGHT SAY

What kinds of arguments will the "little guy's" side make throughout the course of the trial? Here's a rundown of some of the most common approaches.

The opening statement. Opening statements, while often dramatic, are not designed to provide the final arguments the jury will need to decide the case. Lawyers, at this point, are expected to recite the facts that they intend to prove during the trial -- not argue in favor of viewing those facts as persuasive reasons to decide a case one way or the other. (And if one attorney claims that Fact A will be proved, then fails to prove it during the trial, you can bet you'll hear about it from the other side before the jury heads into seclusion to deliberate.)

Expect the defense to say very little at the outset of a criminal trial. There are several reasons for this choice. First of all, the accused's attorney will be unenthusiastic about committing to a position that may have to be abandoned should the State's evidence change. Secondly, the defendant may take advantage of his or her Constitutional rights and -- eventually -- decline to take the stand. If the attorney goes into great detail at the opening statement, the defendant may be unnecessarily limited from a strategic point of view if a later decision not to testify is made. Certain criminal cases look better early on for a defendant than they do halfway through, and occasionally counsel may have to alter his or her strategy on the question of whether or not to place a client on the witness stand.

What the criminal defense lawyer will say, more than likely, is that jurors should keep an open mind, that decency and fairness forbid preconceived approaches to the evidence or the claims of the prosecutor; that the client's indictment itself is not evidence of any wrongdoing, but rather the mechanism used to bring the matter to trial for a verdict. The defense probably will emphasize the heavy burden of proof the State must satisfy in order to attain a conviction, and argue that, no matter what may be presented to the jury, the insufficient or questionable evidence put forth by the prosecutor will not erase all reasonable doubts as to the defendant's innocence, and will compel a decision favorable to his or her client.

So much for the opening statement of the criminal "little guy." The civil suit's "underdog" -- the disabled accident victim, the government employee claiming discrimination, the former patient suing a doctor for malpractice, or any of a hundred other such parties -- is the *plaintiff* now, not the defendant. In the civil setting, the opening statement issuing from this side of the case can be expected to go into a little more detail.

What kind of detail, of course, will depend on the facts that surround the particular case. But some things can be anticipated -- or written off as improbable. For instance, the technique of withholding crucial facts until an important point in the trial -- so familiar to television writers -- is most unlikely to be used in front of a real jury. Study after study indicates that jurors often make an initial decision on their verdict in civil suits by the end of the opening statement, then look for evidence to reinforce initial reactions to the case. Accordingly, the lawyer for the plaintiff usually will showcase the full complement of facts that are unfavorable to the other side, then, later in the trial, set about attempting to prove them forcefully, without any theatrical gimmickry.

Direct examination and exhibits. The criminal defendant's attorney usually must overcome significant obstacles to secure a favorable outcome to the trial, especially during the stage of the trial dedicated to direct examination and exhibits. Because the bulk of the prosecutor's case often rests upon the testimony of courtwise, well-spoken police officers familiar with the methods employed in criminal courts, the defense frequently must come up with ways to make the accused's side sound just as convincing -- or even set up "end runs" around the prosecution that take advantage of strategic or procedural loopholes. Here are some of the most common methods employed.

In many criminal cases, the defense will produce character witnesses. Typically, these are individuals who take the stand with the sole purpose of eliciting sympathy for the accused, and whose testimony often is meaningless when it comes to determining guilt or innocence. Making that determination is, after all, what the jury has been assembled for. An argument can be made for regarding such testimony with a certain degree of skepticism unless the defense can translate the witness' enthusiasm for the accused into tangible facts that pertain to the case.

Cases that involve informers -- such as drug trials -- frequently feature charges by the defense of mistaken identity or entrapment. This is no coincidence. Even if no such procedural problem actually exists, attorneys know that police officers don't disclose their sources and contacts in these cases in open court. Drug cases follow certain patterns; one of them is that arrests usually take place after an undercover identity has been in place for some time, allowing an officer exposure to many dealers. A favorite defense ploy is to try to demonstrate that the officer has made many clandestine drug purchases over a period of months, and, thus, mistakenly arrested the accused long after the crime took place. Because defense counsel is confident an informer will not be produced, the argument can be made that the police officer -- often the only witness in such a case -- inadvertently "fingered" the wrong person. This line of defense can look much more convincing than it actually is. In such a "witness-free" environment, claims of entrapment, too, can take on more weight than they deserve.

In the face of overwhelming evidence, seemingly certain conviction, and unsuccessful attempts to plea bargain (i.e., plead guilty to a lesser offense to avoid trial on a more serious charge the State could pursue), experienced defense lawyers will nevertheless press onward and argue passionately for a verdict of not guilty. Why? Because a good defense lawyer can work wonders -- facts or no facts. If counsel can convince one juror to hold out, can plant in one mind the seeds of doubt, can establish the most tenuous argument that convinces only a single member of the jury that conviction is too harsh a measure, the State must retry the case. That next trial may reopen a once-dim hope of a plea bargain: time passes, the dockets are hopelessly clogged with new cases, witnesses move to other cities, memories fade. This phenomenon, quite common in our legal system, serves as yet another reminder of the validity of this book's central idea: facts don't win cases, people do.

In civil cases, keep a close watch on the vocabulary employed by the attorney representing the side claiming damage or wrongdoing. A skilled advocate knows how to use certain words to enhance a client's position in very subtle -- but time-tested -- ways. For example, in an automobile accident case, the plaintiff's counsel might ask his or her client what happened inside the automobile when the two autos "smashed" together. The word "smashed" conjures up for the jury all sorts of images that may or may not accurately depict the facts of the case. A skilled opponent will object to such terminology, but even then a good lawyer can be expected to have instructed the "little guy" in exactly what words to use on the stand in describing events. These techniques can make very real impressions on a jury.

Cross-examination. In criminal cases, expect defense counsel to probe for discrepancies in the testimony of unfriendly witnesses. If the witness has a criminal record or has turned State's evidence, the focus probably will be on attempts to impeach the person's credibility, or to outline for the jury exactly what deal has been cut in order to enter the testimony. If the defense can portray the witness as untruthful, deceptive, or corrupt, most juries will discount the testimony to some degree. Frequently this is enough to create real doubt about the State's case.

Defense attorneys will often, during cross-examination, demonstrate the prosecution's failure to obtain supporting scientific evidence -- fingerprints, hair samples, fiber specimens, and so forth. While police and prosecutors know that such "lab work" cannot, because of manpower constraints, be obtained in every case, and frequently is unnecessary in crimes with other strong supporting evidence, jurors may be swayed by such arguments. After all, that's the kind of evidence they always talk about on television!

In civil cases, both plaintiff's and defendant's lawyers can be counted on to attempt to discredit the witnesses of the other side. A favorite technique is to demonstrate exactly what a witness has -- and has not -- been coached to testify to by the opposing attorney. Jurors can expect to have the main facts of an issue established with great clarity in direct examination. But seemingly minor details will often be probed relentlessly by opposing attorneys, on the strength of the argument that the "real" story would be just as unclear, contradictory, and chaotic without the aid of a lawyer.

Expert witnesses provide a particular challenge for the lawyer defending the "little guy." Certain approaches are standard procedure, as they have been proven effective time after time. One of these is the "divide and conquer" ploy. Simply stated, the objective is to get adverse expert witnesses to contradict one another, and perhaps even agree with the plaintiff on certain points! If this can be accomplished -- even if the points in dispute seem less than crucial to the case -- the plaintiff's version of events can be bolstered.

Every attorney, of course, hopes to produce facts on cross-examination that are unflattering to the other side's account of things. There are a number of ways to do this, including comparing the witness's direct examination with documents, exhibits, answers to interrogatories, or deposition testimony. People usually don't have photographic memories. Details will differ. Much will be made of this fact during cross-examination, particularly if the issue is one which is integral to the plaintiff's claim of wrongdoing or negligence against the defendant.

Summation. The lawyer for the defense in a criminal trial is usually looking for an acquittal. If that is impossible, a "hung jury" is acceptable. To achieve either goal, the emphasis in summation -- the final argument to the jury -- must be centered upon the idea of "reasonable doubt."

If the facts appear overwhelming, defense counsel will insist that they are contrived and drawn, without real foundation, or misinterpreted altogether. If evidence is substantial, he or she will plead that full scientific data was not assembled -- or assembled incompetently -- and that returning a conviction on such a body of evidence would be a travesty of justice. If a line-up was used, the defense attorney will argue that it was composed suggestively, in order to frame the defendant. If a confession was given, the jury will be told it was involuntary and improperly achieved. If the client has testified, much will be made of the fact that he or she waived a Constitutional right not to do so, and that the client relishes the opportunity to proclaim innocence to all who will listen. If the crime was outrageous or offensive to decency, defense counsel will admit the facts, agree that the act requires punishment, and then, having found a point of agreement with the jury, argue that the real perpetrator is still at large, that the defendant must not be punished for an act he or she did not commit.

A variation on the above may occur in the case where it is common knowledge that a defendant did commit some crime -- but the question before the jury is one of determining exactly what that crime was. In such instances, the jury may be startled to hear the defense proclaim that no circumstances should allow the defendant's walking out of the courtroom with a verdict of not guilty! Such a summation only accepts circumstances as they are (no such verdict will be returned anyway) and, in consonance with other elements in the case, may prevail upon jurors to deliver a more lenient decision. This approach to the summation -- one which takes advantage of a rhetorical surprise and admits damaging facts outright -- may be used in cases where the defendant argues diminished capacity.

Summation in civil cases is less dramatic but just as intricately linked to strategy. Each counsel will supply the "real" answer to those questions purposefully left ambiguous during respective cross-examinations.

The plaintiff's counsel will rarely claim that the defendant is incompetent or malevolent, but rather the author of a significant error for which the law automatically requires compensation. If the defendant is a corporation, it will be referred to in phrases that suggest a large, impersonal entity, and not a collection of human beings who might possess the same emotions or frailties as the plaintiff. If a product allegedly caused the plaintiff's injury, counsel will argue vehemently that a minor change in the product, costing mere pennies per unit, could have prevented the calamity that the plaintiff experienced. Expect the plaintiff's attorney to observe that nothing can make his or her client "whole again," but that the law requires that the jury attempt to do so by returning the proper reward. Such arguments are frequent visitors to the civil courtroom, whether the case involves a lifelong disfigurement and handicap or a highly questionable case of "whiplash" -- or an even less convincing claim. The reason these techniques are used again and again, of course, is that each jury is hearing them for the first time.

A similarly popular technique in the summation of a civil matter is to emphasize the fact that the trial being heard by the jury represents the plaintiff's only day in court; that jury duty is a solemn event; that the client can never return for justice if the jury decide to make a rash judgment. Jurors should recognize this tactic for what it is -- a plea for mercy containing few if any facts relevant to the case.

WHAT THE "BIG GUY'S" SIDE IS LIKELY TO SAY

The opening statement. In a criminal case, the prosecutor will try to open forcefully. As we noted earlier, the words "State" and "People" will be used repeatedly to give the impression that some populist, democratic crusade underlies the position about to be taken. In addition, prosecutors may refer on more than one occasion to the indictment in the case at hand as having been presented by a Grand Jury. This is less out of respect for the institution of the Grand Jury than out of a desire to get the current jury to conclude that other citizens have judged the case already, that the defendant wouldn't have been served with an indictment unless guilty, and that all that remains in the case at hand is the technicality of a verdict favorable to the State. Such things, of course, are never said openly, but they are implied most enthusiastically.

In civil cases, expect all attorneys -- no matter whether their clients are "big," "little," or somewhere in between -- to confront damaging facts head-on in the opening statement. As we learned earlier, juries in civil cases are extremely susceptible to versions of the story that are presented early on; they also are likely to view major changes in that story as evidence of deceptiveness on the part of one or more sides. Accordingly, if a lawyer knows that the opposition has damaging testimony to show the jury, this probably will be mentioned in his or her opening statement. The jury may believe that the attorney is presenting these unflattering facts in order to be fair and honest with them; actually, the objective is to minimize the impact the opposition's "big guns" will have at a later point in the trial.

Direct examination and exhibits. The prosecutor in a criminal case will use exhibits to link the defendant to the crime -- and, perhaps just as important, to reach the jury's emotions in a very subtle but effective way. The actual facts each exhibit demonstrates may not be persuasive, but the presentation of each item certainly can be. Without fingerprints or similarly damaging features, a shotgun or knife *does not prove anything* about the defendant's involvement in a crime. The presence of such weapons in the courtroom, however, heighten the severity of the crime, as do lurid photos of the crime scene. Such exhibits prove a crime was perpetrated and may, in the minds of the jurors, connect the defendant to the act even though no facts warrant that connection.

As exhibits increase in number (and levels of repulsiveness) the skilled prosecutor can "light a fire under the jury," and provoke a strong sentiment that something must be done in the face of such outrages. What could a jury do? Let's see. They could convict the defendant. That's what they could do.

Before the prosecutor can introduce such evidence, however, he or she must demonstrate to the court -- through witnesses -- that the exhibit offered into evidence is the same item that allegedly was found at the scene of the crime. For this reason, the jury may have to endure a number of witnesses whose testimony relates solely to the recovery or, still more boring, storage of the item in question. This testimony is not likely to win any prizes for its inherent entertainment value. Nevertheless, the prosecutor must produce it in order to prove the "chain of custody" of the exhibit, or the item will not be permitted.

As with an attorney in a civil case, the prosecutor will intentionally expose damaging material in the hope of lessening its ultimate impact upon the jury. If a victim has a criminal record, or if an important witness was offered a plea bargain, the State will present these facts in the hope of limiting the effectiveness of the defense attorney during cross-examination -- not because the prosecuting attorney is inherently honest and possessed of a sense of fair play.

How will the "big guy's" attorney conduct direct examination in a civil case? For the most part, the methods are quite similar. One exception can be found in the fact that the "big guy's" lawyer often must attempt to "humanize" a defendant who may be the victim during the trial of stereotypes that accompany businessmen, doctors, landlords, or other "establishment" individuals. One standard procedure might see the attorney referring to his client at the beginning of his testimony as "Mr. Smith," then gradually switching to a first-name basis as the trial progresses. If you begin by listening to what the plaintiff's attorney has to say about "Mr. Smith," you may be convinced easily of his status as a heartless slumlord whose apartments are in dangerously ill repair; but once you get to know "John," you could have difficulty deciding against him -- or so John's attorney hopes.

Of course, this tactic also is used by plaintiff's counsel. The injured plaintiff may initially be referred to as "Mrs. Jones," but odds are that she will, slowly but surely, metamorphose into "Mary."

Cross-examination. On television's criminal dramas, defendants confess their crimes on cross-examination. In real life, they don't. Jurors often conclude that the prosecutor has failed to prove his case if he or she can't get the defendant to admit guilt. The defendant isn't going to admit guilt on the stand, no matter what happened on *L.A. Law* last week, and a savvy prosecutor probably will remind the jury of this fact.

Similarly, a prosecuting attorney will do everything possible to demonstrate that alibi witnesses -- the saviors of the falsely accused on television -- can and do lie shamelessly. If an alibi witness states, six months after the fact, that he can remember watching a situation comedy on a particular Tuesday night with the defendant, that witness better be able to demonstrate total recall about every program watched over the past six months, as well as the company kept during viewing hours. The fact is, alibis supplied long after an arrest, especially when tied to everyday, insignificant events, are less than convincing to a prosecutor. He or she will make every attempt to ensure that they're less than convincing to the jury, as well.

Effective cross-examination in the civil case will follow much the same guidelines as those followed by the attorney representing the "little guy." Questions often will admit only yes-or-no answers, and will not allow the witness to repeat direct testimony. As a general rule, unless he or she is faced with an utterly hopeless case, an experienced attorney will not ask questions during cross-examination to which the answers are unknown. Points will be made in a short, crisp, straightforward fashion, and the witness will not be allowed to soliloquize. Every effort will be made to minimize the defendant's vulnerability to charges of liability or wrongdoing, and to discredit witnesses who help the cause of the opposition.

Summation. A prosecuting attorney in a strong criminal case will acknowledge that the Constitution does in fact guarantee every defendant the right to a fair trial. He or she will continue by observing that it does not afford the accused the right to escape conviction in the face of overwhelming evidence.

If the defense has raised significant doubts about a victim's ability to identify a witness, the prosecutor will highlight the terror and uniqueness that accompanies a criminal act, even one of brief duration. During a crime, he or she will argue, a five second glance can take an eternity.

If the State's witnesses are of questionable character, the prosecutor will try to convince the jury that the law takes its victims as it finds them, and that the background of victims or others involved in the case is irrelevant to the fact that the defendant acted in violation of the law.

The prosecutor must convince all twelve jurors of the defendant's guilt beyond a reasonable doubt. It's a tough job. If the lawyer is an experienced one, he or she will stress that every conflict contains some uncertainty, but that in the case at hand not enough exists to justify an acquittal.

In most civil cases, the plaintiff is required to prove his or her case by a "fair preponderance of the believable evidence." What this means is that the defense is likely to concentrate in summation on the quality of the evidence submitted, rather than the quantity. If a defense attorney can demonstrate that most (or even half) of the plaintiff's evidence is less than believable, he or she has, theoretically, won. A good civil attorney defending a "big guy" will often convince the jury that, because of the weakness of the evidence, the opposition has failed to demonstrate that the event alleged against the defendant was more likely than not to have taken place. If that sounds complicated, it's because it is; but the general idea should be clear. Sometimes the decision will turn on whether or not the plaintiff has proved *enough*, not whether or not anything damaging has been determined.

CHAPTER NINE:
Personal Injury --
What's It Worth?

BEFORE YOU READ THIS CHAPTER...

In personal injury cases, it is essential to secure qualified legal counsel for a professional evaluation of the circumstances a potential plaintiff may face.

If you are contemplating bringing suit against anyone in a personal injury situation, *seek a competent attorney* to assist you in your decisions.

EVALUATING THE CASE

"How much is he suing for?"
"How much is my injury worth?"
These are among the first questions posed to a trial lawyer representing a defendant or plaintiff in a personal injury case.   In each case, there really is no fixed answer. Lawyers consider many factors when advising their clients to offer or accept a particular sum.   These factors can be divided into two categories: non-medical and medical.

NON-MEDICAL FACTORS

As far as money is concerned, the geographic location of a case often is more important than the physical location of the plaintiff's injuries.   Typically, rural verdicts are more conservative than urban ones in cases that are pursued to the bitter end; it follows that settlements, also, are less in the "boondocks" than they are among the "city slickers."   In each state, certain counties are known as high or low verdict jurisdictions to the region's attorneys. What may seem to be an unjustly low award in one area may be quite substantial in another.   It is possible that the plaintiff and his or her attorney may do some "forum shopping," and attempt to file a lawsuit in an area considered to be a high verdict jurisdiction.

In addition to weighing the region's reputation for high or low verdicts, the plaintiff's lawyer must also consider whether the jurisdiction bifurcates (that's legalese for "splits") its cases. When a trial is bifurcated, only the liability issues are heard initially by the jury. If the jury determines that the person the plaintiff is suing is indeed at fault, the trial proceeds on to the second stage -- in which that jury (or another one) hears testimony regarding the extent of the damages suffered, and attempts to determine a fair award.

Obviously, defense attorneys love bifurcated trials. They allow the defendant's side "two bites at the apple." If the defense loses in the liability phase, it can change strategy during the subsequent stage of the trial. Often a plaintiff's injuries will be severe but not visually obvious, which can work to the defense's advantage in the first phase of a bifurcated trial.

In assessing whether or not to push for a settlement, each side of the case must appraise the expertise of the opposition, as well as the competency of the trial judge. Among the questions to be asked are these: Does the opposition lawyer possess a great deal of trial experience? Can he or she make a favorable impression before a jury? Does the judge know how to make proper rulings regarding the evidence? Is the judge regarded as a "plaintiff's judge" or a "defendant's judge"? How does the judge feel about the opposition lawyer? About our side? Will the judge move the case along? Or allow it to drag on tediously, boring and irritating the jury?

Each lawyer also must evaluate the strengths and

weaknesses of the case presented to him or her. Will the judge (or jury) consider the case frivolous? Does one side appear to have an advantage? If so, will the evidence presented be overwhelming or merely marginal? Can the client(s) make a favorable impression upon the jury? How about the witnesses? How much will expert witnesses charge to testify? Are they available upon short notice, or must they be videotaped? Are there any fees that must be paid from the settlement funds (i.e., workers compensation or disability liens)? Have all the medical bills been paid by health insurance? If not, will the doctor or hospital accept a lesser sum? Are there lost wages? Will there be future lost wages? Should these factors be figured into the settlement?

MEDICAL FACTORS

Of course, each side also must review medical factors thoroughly. Obviously, there are many, many questions that accompany the medical side of a personal injury case, each of which is unique. The list that follows is a representative sampling of what an experienced attorney should be attempting to determine before entering into a case.

What is the age and sex of the claimant? What type of injury was sustained? How serious was it? What type of treatment was provided? What was the length of treatment? Was there hospitalization? If so, was it for bed rest, or did it involve sophisticated testing? Which doctors provided treatment, and what are their reputations? Are they regarded as "overtreaters" by colleagues? Was surgery required? Will more be required? What is the current prognosis? Is the current condition something the plaintiff will have to live with for the rest of his or her life? Has a prior injury been aggravated? If so, would that aggravation have occurred even without the present accident's occurrence? Has the plaintiff had similar injuries before (or since) this incident? Will the plaintiff's condition worsen over time? Has there been psychological or psychiatric treatment?

In evaluating the merits of an injury case, each side must ponder the answers to the above questions (and many more like them), then gauge what might be a "fair" -- and, at this point, completely hypothetical -- settlement figure for use by the clients as a guide to what the case is "worth." The difficulty arises when counsel is unable to explain the disparity in "worth" between what seem to clients to be similar cases. How, for instance, is an attorney diplomatically to inform a client that his or her case is worth less money than a relative's very nearly identical experience because the client will be perceived as offensive by the jury, while Aunt Irene was not?

DIFFERENT TYPES OF
INJURY CASES

"Soft tissue" injuries. The "soft tissue" case is the most common injury litigated in our court system. It's

frequently seen in automobile cases, as well as in cases in which a plaintiff sustains an injury in a fall.

What is a "soft tissue" injury? Typically, the term refers to a sprain or strain of muscles or ligaments. While the terms "sprain" and "strain" possess different technical meanings, lawyers use the terms interchangeably to describe stretching or tearing of various parts of the body.

For example, in a "routine" motor vehicle accident, a plaintiff may complain of pain to the cervical (neck) and lumbo-sacral (lower back) regions. X-rays don't reveal any kind of fracture, but the neck and back pain persists. That pain may emanate from damage done to the muscles adjacent to the spinal column, and such damage would be classified as a "soft tissue" injury. Obviously, a physician's method and duration of treatment of such an injury would figure strongly into any decent lawyer's assessment of the case.

Treatment for soft tissue injuries often follows a predictable pattern. In fact, it's common in some jurisdictions to find a doctor "specializing" in the treatment of such accident-related injuries in case after case. After a while, an experienced attorney can almost write the doctor's report!

Most "soft tissue" cases will fall within a predictable settlement range that will be quite familiar to qualified local counsel.

Fractures. Broken bones are often unfortunate byproducts of a serious collision or fall. In determining the value of a fracture case, an attorney must evaluate the location and extent of the fracture, virtually always doing so in conjunction with the evaluation of a physician.

A fracture may be either "simple" or "compound." The distinction is quite straightforward, though a little tough to take if you've just gotten done eating: a "simple" fracture is one in which the broken bone does not protrude through the skin, while a "compound" fracture does. There are a great many more detailed subdivisions of fractures. The two major distinctions, though, probably encompass enough for our purposes.

The number and type of fractures, their severity, and their treatment, together with the physician's diagnosis, will determine the potential value of each case. A fractured ankle may heal easily in one instance, but cause chronic discomfort and permanent disability in another. The plaintiff who breaks seven ribs may be able to perform normal activities relatively quickly, while one who has fractured a shoulder may never regain full movement. Usually, the passage of time assists an attorney in evaluating the severity of a fracture case.

Disc cases. Because many accidents involve injury to the neck and back regions, disc cases are common occurrences. Broadly speaking, such cases usually refer to a bulging or herniated disc that may touch a spinal nerve, leaving a patient with a "pins-and-needles" sensation or numb feeling in the arms or legs.

If sophisticated medical tests demonstrate the presence of a bulging or herniated disc, a lawyer's first question to the physician probably will concern whether or not surgery is necessary. Disc cases involving surgery usually are settled for more money than those in which surgery is not advised or is refused by the patient. If surgery is undertaken, the degree of success bears heavily on the eventual worth of the case: obviously, the less successful the result, the more "valuable" the case. Even when surgery is successful, however, the patient may never return to a lifestyle as active as the one enjoyed before the accident that occasioned the surgery.

Scar cases. Scars and disfigurements are highly subjective cases, and will vary in value dramatically from one individual to another. A facial scar on a little girl may have a greater potential impact than an identical scar on a middle-aged man, and a scar on a fair-skinned person may be more noticeable than a similar mark on a swarthy one.

Once lawyers have answered the relevant questions surrounding a scar case, which include the sex and age of the injured party, as well as whether or not the scar can be expected to improve over time, an estimate as to the case's value can be made. Scar cases usually are settled out of court, as neither side is enthusiastic about presenting a subjective and, usually, unpredictable case to a jury. Another reason to settle quickly is the relative scarcity of disputed facts about the actual injury in a "typical" scar case. No one fakes a scar, and while its worth may be open to question, its presence is not.

Amputation cases. While cases involving amputation feature obvious injury and pain, some will have more value than others. Obviously, the loss of a fingertip constitutes a "weaker" case than the loss of a finger.

The type and extent of the amputation, coupled with such variables as the plaintiff's age, sex, marital status, and occupation, will determine the value of the case. In major amputation cases, the physical and emotional suffering are obviously significant -- and the corresponding settlement offers or jury awards will probably be significant as well.

Catastrophic injuries. The most common and devastating catastrophic injuries encountered by trial attorneys involve paraplegia (in which both lower limbs are paralyzed) and quadriplegia (in which all four limbs are paralyzed). Such injuries are prevalent in swimming pool cases and motorcycle accidents, where severe spinal cord damage is often incurred.

Obviously, in these cases, the pain and suffering associated with a defendant's purported negligence are staggering. The medical costs and lost wage claims can be overwhelming when extensive long-term medical and financial care is required. Such catastrophic injury cases usually are resolved, where sufficient funds exist, in structured settlements that take into account the projected years of medical care and related costs. Such settlements often are higher than wrongful death claims pursued by the estate of a plaintiff of a similar age, marital status, and occupation.

Where liability is uncontested, be wary of the attorney who boasts of the size of a previous award in such a case. These cases, in and of themselves, have significant value, and usually require a truly incompetent lawyer to generate an unimpressive settlement or judgment.

MEETING THE OPPOSITION'S DOCTOR: FACE TO FACE WITH "THE ENEMY"

Most personal injury cases will involve an examination of the plaintiff by a doctor selected by the opposition. This is not likely to be an experience anticipated eagerly by any litigant.

In order to eliminate, or at least minimize, the client's anxiety, as well as make the examination as profitable as possible for all involved, most lawyers will prepare a letter of instruction for the client who must undergo such an examination.

This letter combines specific instructions for the physical examination with some good advice for the purposes of the trial.   It should be forwarded to you well before the examination, usually about two weeks prior to the date set.

A letter of instruction does not replace the need to consult with your attorney about the examination, but can serve as a tangible restatement of objectives before a difficult encounter.

The following is an example of a standard letter of instruction.

Dear Client,

Since you are about to be examined by a doctor on behalf of the defendant, you should be well prepared to discuss your injury with the examining physician. Remember that this examination and the doctor's testimony may be used at trial. Because the events in the examination are important to your case, you should probably review thoroughly the following suggestions.

PREPARING FOR THE EXAMINATION

Remember that the doctor is paid by the defendant. You do not have to pay anything for your visit. Quite to the contrary, the doctor is working *for the other side* and is interested in minimizing the physical problems you have. The doctor is not your friend.

Be prompt. Show up slightly early for the appointment, even though you can expect the doctor to be overbooked, and to make you wait some time before being examined.

TALKING TO THE DOCTOR

Do not discuss blame. Do not discuss how your physical problem came about. *Remember that your conversations with this doctor are not privileged,* and can be used in court. The doctor's job is to estimate the extent of the injury -- not to decide who was at fault.

Tell the doctor about each and every complaint you have. Let the other side worry about whether or not it was caused by the events at issue in your case. Start at the very top of your head and work your way down, outlining every injury or pain you feel -- no matter how minor it may appear to you. This doctor's job is to downplay your injuries when reporting to the defendant -- don't help him or her in that job! If outlining everything that's wrong means sounding like a complainer, don't be afraid to complain! Your complaints are legitimate.

Tell the doctor how any pain you feel affects your daily life. If you were unable to work after the accident, say so. If you've been limited in your performance of household chores, forced to drop out of the bowling league, assigned to lighter duties at work, or even disappointed in your sex life since the incident in question, say so.

GENERAL GUIDELINES

Tell the truth. Do not hide information about previous accidents or injuries. Such information should not be considered by you to be damaging to your case.

Be polite and let the physician work. Even if you do not like the doctor, allow the examination to proceed. Unless you are asked to submit to some highly unusual test, comply with all instructions.

Always bear in mind that the doctor's job is to determine *how little* -- not how much -- you are hurt. Work with him or her, but remember that your goals are completely separate.

Meet with our office two days prior to the scheduled examination for a final review of instructions.

I hope the above instructions will be helpful to you. Remember to stay calm, be polite, and always pay attention to what is happening during your visit.

Sincerely,

John Smith
Attorney At Law

CHAPTER TEN:
Insurance

EVERYBODY HAS IT, NOBODY UNDERSTANDS IT: THE MODERN INSURANCE DILEMMA

Why do insurance companies pay you less than it costs to fix your damaged car? What are the implications to your insurance coverage if you plead guilty to a motor vehicle accident ticket? Why do insurance carriers pay out money to the injured -- but negligent -- child who runs a bicycle into the side of your car? What is the sense of an insurance company offering to defend you in court, then refusing to pay the judgment entered against you when you lose?

In this chapter, we'll examine these and other problems that relate to the often confusing world of insurance policies.

YOUR DUTY TO THE INSURANCE COMPANY

All insurance policies require that parties give timely notice of the accident or other relevant incident to the insurance carrier. This notice is required because the company must quickly investigate the claim, secure witnesses, and determine the cause and extent of your liability.

If you don't inform your carrier of the occurrence you expect them to cover, and if the insurance company can show that your failure to do so affected its ability to defend the lawsuit arising out of the matter, you may find yourself without insurance. If the company makes a successful attempt to disclaim coverage, the other party in the suit could proceed against you personally and, conceivably, attach your assets.

Notify your insurance company by telephone of all relevant facts immediately. Then write a letter that outlines the incident, and make three copies: one for your insurance company's headquarters office, one for your insurance agent, and one for yourself. Be sure to include your name, address, work and home telephone numbers, and policy number. Also provide as much detail about the incident as possible, being sure to mention the setting, the actual events, contact information on any witnesses, and the activities of any investigating bodies, such as the police or fire department. If you know of the existence of any photographs taken at the scene, outline who has them and explain how that person can be contacted.

Don't provide any description -- written or oral -- to the other person's insurance company or private investigator. Such a description will almost certainly be used against you at a later date to minimize any claim on your part.

There are certain exceptions to this. If you are involved in a minor auto accident claim, for instance, and have not been injured, but must deal with extensive damage to your car -- damage that's clearly the fault of the other side -- there may be no legal conflict at all. The other person's insurance company might offer to pay an attractive amount, and you might determine that the cash at stake does not warrant the hiring of an attorney. In instances such as these, you'll want to cooperate with the opposition's insurance company; but if you do so, be sure to give written -- not oral and recorded -- statements. This minimizes the possibility of any misstatement, as you can review your account closely before sending it off, saving a copy for your records. Be wary of any claim forms you're asked to complete in this scenario: don't draw diagrams, estimate distances, or provide contact information on any individual with whom you have not spoken in detail about the incident and obtained permission to disclose such data.

If you are served with a summons and complaint, call both your agent and your insurance carrier immediately. Your agent will often request that you send him the complaint, which he or she will then forward to the insurance company. Always keep a photocopy of both your transmittal letter and the documents for your records. If you do not hear from your insurance company within thirty days, contact both your agent and your insurance company. Follow the same procedure if you are instructed to send the materials directly to the insurance company.

When your carrier finally receives the summons and complaint, it will either settle the matter quickly or refer it to counsel for defense. Insurance companies use either their own in-house attorneys to defend their customers (known as "insureds"), or refer cases to outside independent counsel, who then bill the carrier. Whichever counsel represents you, it is your duty to cooperate in all elements of the litigation process, including answering interrogatories, submitting to depositions, and even participating in the trial if no settlement is forthcoming. If you withhold cooperation, your insurance coverage can be denied. Be sure your attorney knows how to contact you at all times.

Consult with the attorney before pleading guilty to any citation, particularly a motor vehicle citation. It is often possible to obtain a reservation from the court that your plea be inadmissible in any future civil dispute.

Remember that your insurance company and the lawyer representing it are the only entities that can enter settlement negotiations. You cannot attempt to negotiate a compromise on your own; if you read your policy carefully, you will almost certainly find a provision stating that coverage can be negated if an insured attempts to compromise or resolve a claim without the carrier's permission.

When your insurance company has made a damage reimbursement payment to you, it has a right to file suit through its attorneys in your name to recover money paid to you. For example, if someone has damaged your car through their negligent driving, your auto insurance carrier can sue that person to recover the full amount it paid you to have the car repaired. Your insurance company will require that you assist in that recovery. If you refuse, it's conceivable that your carrier can file suit against you for breach of your insurance contract, and claim that you are bound to repay the money they supplied for repairs.

Obviously, it is in your interest to assist your carrier's

efforts. While the litigation that accompanies insurance matters is often time-consuming and inconvenient, this is really a small price to pay for the security achieved.

YOUR CARRIER'S DUTY TO YOU

Your insurance company, in automobile or property damage situations, has a duty to make a quick and reasonable settlement with you once it has been notified of the claim. The carrier can require that your property or auto be appraised by several companies before offering you a settlement; typically, the final sum offered will be an average of the various appraisals, less any deductible you may have on your policy. The value of your damaged property normally will not be its original price, but can be expected to depreciate. Damaged items are valued at the time of the loss, not at the time of purchase.

Accordingly, when an insurance company must determine the value of an automobile, its age and condition are weighed into the final settlement. Most people don't think of their cars as being worth a certain sum that declines over time. If you have a good car, chances are that, rather than ticking off a specific dollar amount, you consider your car to be worth exactly one similar automobile on the dealer's showroom. However, if yours is, say, four or five years old, and is destroyed in an accident, your settlement check will not come anywhere near the sum you'll need to purchase another vehicle.

Once you accept your insurance carrier's settlement check, you waive your rights to obtain a higher sum from the responsible party. Only your insurance company can institute a suit against that individual, although you may receive a portion of the final award or settlement if your insurance company sues not only for the amount paid out to you, but also for your deductible.

In some cases, you will be entitled to the use of a rental car while repairs are being made; check your policy to see whether or not it includes rental coverage. If it doesn't, it's a good idea to try to get such coverage, as the premium is comparatively inexpensive and the extra service provided very convenient. Even minor repairs take time, especially if parts must be ordered from remote locations. The cost of car rental insurance is usually a fraction of what might otherwise be spent securing temporary transportation.

WHAT HAPPENS
IF YOU'RE SUED

In situations in which you are sued for something covered under your policy, your insurance company must provide you with an attorney at its expense. That lawyer will handle the entire defense of your claim.

Your carrier is only responsible for making payment on claims that do not exceed your policy limits. Insurance policies are routinely written to incorporate a per-person and per-occurrence limit. An example of this might be a policy paying up to $50,000 per person, but not more than $100,000 per occurrence.

Under such a policy, if an injured party has a claim worth $70,000, your carrier would only be responsible for the first $50,000; you would have to make up the difference out of your own pocket if the individual collected the full amount. This is why insurance companies will inquire, at the outset, as to the plaintiff's demand. If the other side responds with a figure in excess of your policy limits, your company must advise you, so you can engage (at your expense!) a lawyer to represent you in conjunction with the carrier's counsel.

Because the attorneys engaged by insurance companies usually specialize in trial work, it's unlikely that "your" lawyer would supersede the attorneys formulating your defense through the carrier. On the other hand, engaging such personal counsel in these instances can be a good idea. He or she could review the case and offer suggestions to assist in the defense of your suit -- and, perhaps most importantly, serve as your advocate where the sums not covered by your policy are concerned.

If a plaintiff offers to settle for a figure within the policy limits, and the carrier refuses to pay that figure, some states have held that the insurance company must be considered responsible for the entire award ultimately determined, regardless of its size. The argument is that a carrier should not jeopardize the insured person's assets by gambling that its position will be accepted by the jury. Ask about the relevant statute in your case.

It is common for plaintiff's lawyers to make initial demands bearing no relationship to the "real value" of the case. Such exaggeration allows for substantial movement during settlement negotiations. It is not unusual to see a $50,000 demand wind up as a $6,000 case.

A carrier's obligations toward you do have limitations. Insurance policies afford coverage for negligent acts, not intentional ones. If you accidentally strike another person's car, you're covered. If you wake up one morning and decide that it would be fun to ram your Honda into your next-door neighbor's VW Beetle, you're not. It may sound flippant, but lawyers are quite cognizant of the distinction between intentional and unintentional acts, and may make much of "suspicious" circumstances.

If, for instance, you are sued by someone for hitting their car, and you have a great deal of money, you may find the opposition planning to argue that you acted intentionally -- in order to receive a larger award or settlement than the insurance company could provide! In such a situation, your side would have to cope not only with potential compensatory damages being awarded (in order to fix the car you wrecked), but also with punitive damages (in order to make sure you're suitably chastised about the incident).

If you are sued in this way, or if you are sued under a set of facts which fall outside of your policy's coverage, your carrier may defend you under a "reservation of rights." In essence, what this means is that your carrier will defend you, but may not pay if a sizable judgment is entered against you. If you receive a letter outlining a "reservation of rights," secure counsel immediately and review the details thoroughly before doing anything.

If your carrier settles the plaintiff's case, the other side will have to provide a release and a stipulation of the suit's dismissal to the insurance company. These documents indicate formally that the matter has been resolved, and prevent your adversary from relitigating the claim against you.

If a verdict is entered against you, and if your carrier pays that award, the other counsel will provide a warrant that the verdict has been satisfied. This document, which is filed with the court, is very important. It indicates that the matter has been resolved and that you bear no further financial obligation. If you were trying to sell your house, but could not produce a warrant after participating in a high-visibility lawsuit, the prospective buyer could rightfully refuse to purchase your home out of a concern that your adversary could enforce a judgment by compelling the sale of your home.

Once your case has been resolved, you can request copies of these documents from your carrier or from the court.

UMBRELLA INSURANCE

Insurance companies restrict the amount of primary liability coverage they will write for individuals. What this means is that you may not be able to insure your house, car, or business as fully as you might wish under one policy. Secondary coverage, which allows you to extend additional coverage to a given area, is referred to as umbrella coverage, and can be purchased at comparatively low premium rates.

Umbrella coverage comes into play only after the primary policy has been paid to your adversary. Let's assume that you have automobile coverage which will pay up to $300,000 per person. A verdict is entered against you for $350,000. Your primary policy would pay the claimant $300,000, and your secondary policy would pay the balance.

If you decide to obtain umbrella insurance, you must notify the carrier providing it at the same time you notify your primary carrier of any incident relevant to your insurance coverage. Be sure to inform each carrier of the other's role, and to provide relevant contact details. Once this has been done, the umbrella carrier will monitor your case.

WHY YOU CAN BE SUED
FOR SOMETHING
YOU DIDN'T DO

You are liable not only for your own actions, but for careless or negligent deeds of those individuals under your control. If, for example, your stockboy improperly sweeps your store's floor, you, as owner, can be sued if someone slips and breaks a bone. You, the owner, are known as a "principal" -- the stockboy is considered an "agent." A woman who has broken her ankle on your improperly swept floor can opt to sue you, the stockboy, or both of you.

In such a situation, your insurance policy should cover both you and your "agent." It is obviously important for you to know whether or not your "agent" is being sued for a negligent act for which you may also be liable. Timely notice to your carrier will insure coverage.

Normally, you will not be responsible for the intentional misdeeds of an employee or similar subordinate -- unless you order, approve, or acquiesce in those deeds. If you know of intentional wrongdoing on the part of an "agent," you must inform your carrier quickly to protect yourself.

A different, but related, scenario is one in which an individual whose skills you engage to perform a specific task or series of tasks -- an "independent contractor" -- is involved in an accident or potentially negligent act. How does such a person differ from an employee or "agent"? The contractor utilizes his or her own expertise and procedures in accomplishing the task. While you pay for the services, you don't control the time or method of his or her operations. Accordingly, your liability will differ.

Let's say you hire a plumber to install a water heater. The plumber performs the services incorrectly, your heater explodes, and a visitor is injured.

Initially, you may be responsible, because the incident occurred on your property. You, however, did not exercise control and supervision over the contractor -- who used his own particular knowledge and skill to attempt to install the heater. Therefore, you would be entitled to indemnification from the contractor, because the *primary* negligence was his -- he actually caused the explosion. You would be "vicariously liable" because you hired him.

As long as the contractor had sufficient insurance coverage, his carrier would be responsible to the injured person for the entire ultimate damage award. On the other hand, if the contractor did not have insurance, or lacked sufficient insurance, the injured person would look to you for all or part of the award the the jury might enter against you and the contractor.

Assuming such a situation actually did develop, your insurance company could attempt to recover from the uninsured or underinsured contractor the money that it paid to the injured visitor. (It goes without saying that if *you* don't have insurance to cover such a scenario, you're probably in serious trouble.)

Regardless of your personal evaluation of the person you believe to be at fault in any accident or other cause of litigation, inform your carrier of the relevant facts immediately.

INTERSPOUSAL AND INTERFAMILY MATTERS

In the past, courts routinely precluded spouses from asserting auto accident and other negligent claims against their mates. The theory was that such suits fostered marital disharmony. Children, too, were prevented from initiating such actions against their parents.

Now, however, many states permit this kind of litigation. Jurors still view these kinds of claims with skepticism, however, and the verdicts that are returned tend to be of low value. While many courts will issue specific instructions that such lawsuits are permissible, jurors usually recognize that the action would, in all likelihood, not exist without the presence of insurance coverage. Very little sympathy accompanies these verdicts, and unimpressive awards are quite common.

CLAIMS AGAINST THE GOVERNMENT

Over the past twenty years or so, a number of federal and state laws have been passed that allow greater latitude in the area of pursuing claims of personal injury against governmental entities. The field of law addressing this area, however, remains extremely complex and, to the lay individual, quite confusing. Certain situations in certain states will lead to legitimate claims, while others will not.

If you are injured as a result of a negligent act committed by a governmental employee, contact an attorney immediately. Rigid guidelines exist in these types of cases, and if they are not followed your claim can be barred.

NO-FAULT INSURANCE

When no-fault insurance first came into fashion, it was

viewed as the cure-all to the bloated civil case docket. Medical bills and lost wages, the argument went, would be paid expeditiously, claims would decrease, and all would be well in the troubled world of accident law.

Unfortunately, reality has had other ideas. Lawsuits haven't declined; insurance premiums haven't plummetted. Some of the states that adopted no-fault so enthusiastically have since abandoned it as a futile approach.

If you live in a no-fault insurance state, remember that all medical bills and lost wage claims must be submitted to your carrier immediately after the accident. Forward all medical bills to the adjuster; your accident will be identified by date and claim number. Your carrier will probably be required to pay you within a certain time period, but usually must only issue funds on those bills that are reasonable, necessary, and submitted in a timely manner.

You may be required by your carrier to submit to an independent medical exam to determine whether or not continued treatment of a physical problem should be covered under your policy. These exams are typically required in whiplash cases, where treatment can, on occasion, continue well after the initial medical problem has subsided.

If the independent examination indicates that no further treatment is necessary, your carrier has the right to terminate payments. If that occurs, and both you and your physician still feel strongly that the treatment should continue, your only real option is to continue the treatment and sue the carrier for reimbursement. Once you decide on that course, it's up to the court to decide on the legitimacy of your requests for further treatment.

UNINSURED MOTORIST CLAIMS

If you look at your policy closely, you'll probably notice something called an uninsured motorist's endorsement. This portion of your policy provides protection in the event of your being injured by an uninsured driver. In such a situation, you are permitted to recover damages for your injuries by filing a claim against your own insurance company. That claim is then processed through an arbitrator.

Your insurance company can require that you submit to a medical examination in this situation, which would be tendered to the arbitrator for review. After the arbitrator has had a chance to go over all the evidence, a decision will be rendered. While the methods of an arbitrator may be somewhat more informal than those of a jury or judge, the decision in your case has exactly the same effect as a court verdict.

Frequently, uninsured motorist claims result from hit-and-run accidents. Your carrier will attempt to locate the driver responsible for the accident and pursue its rights to sue in your name and recover the money paid to you.

INFANT SETTLEMENTS

Whenever a claim is put forth on behalf of an injured child, that suit is instituted in the name of the child's guardian, typically one of the parents. Any settlement or verdict entered in favor of a minor must usually be placed in an interest-bearing account overseen by an appropriate governmental entity. Before the guardian can withdraw funds from that account, he or she must apply to that official, so that the proper precautions can be taken to insure that the funds are used for the child's benefit (for example, to pay educational bills).

If your child is injured and is entitled to recover damages, you will probably be encouraged to settle out of court by the other side. If a settlement is reached, however, a court must approve the final arrangements, as the welfare of a minor is involved. If the agreement is accepted by the court, both the guardian and, if possible, the child, will be examined under oath. The idea is to make sure the guardian understands that, once the settlement is approved, the matter cannot be litigated again, even if the child's injuries worsen or fail to make the expected improvements.

Infant settlements can vary widely. If the injury is severe, and if liability is absolute, structured settlements (that is, settlements paid out over time) are frequently employed. Because the injured child often does not need large cash sums, but rather continuing funds to deal with ongoing medical bills, money is often channelled through an annuity. This allows funds to accumulate, so that much larger payments are made over a period of years.

Where liability is questionable, but there is still substantial damage, insurance companies may attempt to settle on a single lump sum in infant injury cases. Usually this is to avoid the possibility of an unfavorable jury verdict should the evidence at trial turn in the child's favor. This is why your carrier may pay what seems to you to be an unreasonable amount to a child who drives a bicycle into your car, leaving you no time to avoid an accident. The $7500 or so paid out to a child with a broken leg may seem excessive to you -- after all, it was "the child's fault" -- but may actually represent a realistic compromise that is much more prudent than allowing the case to be heard by a jury.

CHAPTER ELEVEN:
Five Bucks and a Blood Test to Get Married, a Fortune to Get a Divorce

GREED, PASSION, CONFLICT, AND FABRICATION: THE JOYS OF DIVORCE COURT

Matrimonial law as a whole is a vengeful, irrational, and often bloodstained beast that has no equal in the legal jungle.

Nowhere is greed, passion, and fabrication more prevalent than in the matrimonial courtroom. Nowhere will the incompetent and inexperienced attorney have a better opportunity to exploit the bitterness, weakness, or instability of the client. Nowhere is the potential greater for catastrophic emotional or personal losses -- especially if counsel fails to provide an objective appraisal of the case, an all-too-common occurrence. In the end, the only real winners in this sad specialty are the attorneys.

A contested divorce provides one of the worst imaginable environments for establishing the facts of a case. As virtually every lawyer or judge who has any matrimonial experience can attest, lies are quite common in the divorce court: the conflict that does not feature at least one major lie per litigant is rare. Maintaining your balance in a court setting can be difficult in the best of times. During the ordeal of a divorce, to do so is very nearly impossible.

In this chapter we'll examine a number of areas that can be troublesome for the participants on both sides of a matrimonial case, and we'll try to highlight some solutions to the legal problems most litigants encounter during this turbulent and very sensitive period of their lives.

CUSTODY

Issue Number One is usually what happens to the kids.

Before you do anything rash -- including, but not limited to, spending vast amounts of money trying to win custody -- take a couple of minutes to examine the environment in which the question of custody ultimately will be resolved.

In this area, as in others, the "practical truth" on which the case will be decided will usually outweigh what one might consider to be the "real facts" necessary to produce a "fair" decision. Your definition of "fair" is very likely to be different from the court's.

It doesn't matter what your brother tells you. It doesn't matter what your friends tell you. And (ready for this?) it doesn't matter what your attorney tells you, either. When it comes to custody, the woman will win in the vast majority of cases. In virtually all situations where custody is an issue, most judges will side with the mother in resolving the emotionally charged question of who lives with whom after the divorce. There are only two exceptions to this general rule.

If the children are old enough, intelligent enough, and articulate enough to make their own determination about where and with whom they wish to reside, the father's cause may get a boost. How old is old enough? The standard employed by most judges is usually somewhere between ten and twelve years of age. If children at this age level can coherently advise the Court of their desire to live with the father, a reasonable chance exists that those wishes will be respected.

The other exception involves those situations in which the father and his attorney can prove, beyond doubt, that the mother is unfit. A judge will seriously consider awarding custody to the father if the mother can be shown to have: abused the children; exposed them to unreasonable dangers; or been guilty of some other gross dereliction of her duties.

If you're a father about to enter a divorce proceeding, and you want to win custody of your children, take a close look at the circumstances surrounding your case. If your request can't receive realistic consideration under either of the categories outlined above, it's a good bet that you've already lost the battle.

Many matrimonial attorneys, who know full well that these are the "rules of the road," will counsel a father in a divorce case that he has "a shot" at winning custody, and that the only way to win custody is to fight for it. In the absence of the two conditions cited above, the attorney may offer a number of reasons to pursue the fight, including the totally irrelevant one that the father is "clearly a better parent."

If the mother is a reasonably competent mother, and if the children involved either do not meet the "age cut-off" requirement or are unlikely to speak up in court in an effort to win the right to live with their father, there is little point in pursuing a custody fight.

It is suggested by the authors of this book that any father involved in matrimonial litigation seek a second opinion if he is advised by his attorney to pursue a battle over custody rights. These fights can consume thousands upon thousands of dollars and offer as their only consolation the dubious one of expensive, rather than inexpensive, defeat.

In recent years, a number of articles have been written heralding the coming of "men's rights" in this area. *Don't bet on it.* The typical judicial approach to divorce in general and custody in particular is a simple one: continue doing what's been done for years. That means Mom usually wins.

To be sure, there are some states which utilize the standard which requires the judge to determine the "best interests of the child." This, however, almost invariably results in the decision that continuing to live with the mother is in the child's best interest. Far from initiating a sweeping re-examination of an old problem, this practice usually results in an affirmation of the mother's prerogatives in questions of custody.

JOINT CUSTODY

Joint custody is usually more of an optimistic euphemism than a realistic description of a post-divorce domestic arrangement.

Actual, workable joint custody is a *very* rare occurrence. Much more common is the pattern of one parent maintaining sole custody, and another being granted reasonable and liberal visitation. In the few instances where two parents *do* establish guidelines that allow legitimate joint custody to take place, there's usually some unique element to the situation -- for instance, residences located within easy walking distance of one another -- that's virtually impossible to repeat in someone else's domestic life.

VISITATION

Although custody is generally awarded to the mother, most divorce settlements will feature some kind of visitation arrangement that allows the non-custodial parent to participate on a regular basis in the ongoing life and growth of the children. Obviously, it is preferable to work out the details of the visitation question on an informal, "out-of-court" basis. It's a rare judge who will not recognize this and urge the parties to determine the particulars on their own.

In working out your visitation schedule -- no matter what your status with regard to custody rights -- try to remember that while you are, in one sense, negotiating with an adversary, you are also determining what the child "gets" out of the agreement, as well.

If you hold custody rights, think seriously about being as generous as possible in your arrangements with the non-custodial parent. Be realistic about the consequences of exposing your children to constant bickering over when visits are to take place. All too often, children are used as pawns in personality conflicts between divorced parents. A genuinely fair and workable schedule with your ex-spouse will be easier on everyone involved than an unrealistic arrangement which you feel represents a "win."

Keeping this in mind, a typical visitation schedule might run as follows.

Non-custodial parent will have visitation with the child...

● every other weekend from Friday at 6:00 pm to Sunday at 6:00 pm

● every other major holiday, on a year-to-year alternating schedule

● on the non-custodial parent's birthday

● for a predetermined period of time on the child's birthday

Other features that could be worked into the above agreement include a block of time during the non-custodial parent's vacation (regardless of whether that vacation is two weeks during the summer or six weeks during the course of the year), and appropriate weekday and telephone visitation.

The schedule can vary depending on the age of the child. If, for example, the child is one year old, telephone visitation would not be relevant. If the non-custodial parent does not have facilities necessary for overnight care of a very young child, overnight visits might be inappropriate for the time being. If an older child participates in outside activities (excluding those designed deliberately to interfere with visitation, of course), some adjustment of the schedule may be in order. A typical example of such a compromise might involve a child who participates in a soccer league. In this case, the non-custodial parent could drive the child to and from practice and perhaps attend occasional league games.

If either parent feels, after attempting to implement a schedule such as the one outlined above, that establishing a workable visitation arrangement is impossible without intervention by some third party, there is still one more avenue open before a formal request to the judge. This is the possibility of having a mutual friend (or even a professional arbitrator) mediate the dispute. Though there will be the difficulties that accompany any arbitration process, attempt at all costs to resolve the problem independent of the judge.

By staying out of the courtroom, you can take a major step toward avoiding the trauma of a fight over visitation rights -- a fight that, again, no one in the family is likely to "win."

DISTRIBUTION OF ASSETS

Although a number of standards exist and will vary from state to state, some general tendencies exist among divorce courts when it comes to property allocation.

The two main approaches are known as the *community property standard* and the *equitable distribution standard.*

In most of the states that use the community property standard, community property is taken to mean that all the couple's possessions are divided equally, 50-50 -- no matter who works and who doesn't.

In an equitable distribution state, however, the approach is different. Theoretically, each property settlement under this standard is measured according to each partner's contribution to the relationship: if the wife works at home, makes $100,000 a year, and takes care of the children, she can expect more out of the settlement than her husband who makes $15,000 a year and shares in no domestic duties.

In evaluating either standard, however, the question remains: What constitutes property? The answers vary dramatically. Some states will consider all items acquired by the parties from the time of the marriage until the time of separation (or the filing of a Complaint for Divorce); others will take into account items acquired before the marriage; some even establish complicated standards to determine whether or not an asset entered "common usage" over the course of the couple's time together. Check with your lawyer for the details in your state.

One topic usually of great interest to someone involved in a divorce concerns the home in which the family (and, more pertinently, a child) has lived. Assuming that the family owns the home in question, the standard in this case is a very reliable one, and appropriate in most divorces: the custodial parent usually will remain in the home until the youngest child born of the marriage reaches his or her eighteenth birthday, at which point the house is sold and the net proceeds divided according to the terms of the prior arrangements for division of assets.

It may seem "fair" for the non-custodial party's attorney to make a strong argument against this arrangement. After all, the custodial parent has use of the assets of the non-custodial parent at no cost whatsoever!

A more realistic assessment, however, and one the court is very likely to make, is that the custodial parent is maintaining real estate and related assets not only for the benefit of both parties, but also so that the child may continue to live in the home in a style as close as possible to the domestic environment that existed before the separation. Clearly, this objective is a legitimate one, and (though it may seem "unfair"), one which outweighs a valid claim of the non-custodial parent. When other factors are weighed in (the fact that, because of mortgage payments, the net value of the house usually increases; the general tendency of real estate to appreciate over time; the custodial parent's status as a "good tenant"; and certain tax advantages), most courts will have no problem adhering to the standard arrangement.

Examine very closely the advice you get from your attorney in the area of property distribution. If you are deeply enamored of the 1979 Flake-O-Matic Toaster you bought together, and your lawyer tells you you should "go to the mat" over the question, do yourself a favor and figure out whether or not the fees you'll be paying him or her exceed the cost of simply replacing the item. An honest attorney won't encourage you to waste time and money divvying up knick-knacks; others will prey on your desire to maintain some contact with a former period in your life.

TAXES

Taxes underpin virtually every decision in a divorce in one way or another. Unfortunately, many judges who handle matrimonial cases are either not up-to-date on current tax law, or too busy to notice the ramifications of tax-related issues in a divorce. Some, sad to say, are simply uninterested in the effect that their judgments will have on a litigant's tax liability. This is why it's important to select an attorney who is well-versed not only in matrimonial law, but also in the potential tax effects of alimony, child support, and property distribution.

Make sure you select an attorney, either on a primary or advisory basis, who is familiar not only with the ramifications of Federal tax matters such as the capital gains tax and alimony and child support matters, but also with state tax requirements, or other tax questions peculiar to the jurisdiction in which the litigants are located. It should be obvious that, because tax law is an extremely confusing, complicated, and often contradictory subject, litigants should not attempt to "wing it" in this area by avoiding hiring qualified counsel. (Of course, if you're very knowledgeable in tax law, or have a strong accounting background, you may want to see if you can make sense of the principal questions. Then again, you may not.)

To appreciate what your tax liabilities are likely to be, it's a good idea to go over some of the fundamental principles that underlie most divorce judgments. For one thing, alimony is, in many cases, forever -- or at least required until the party receiving it remarries or dies. Child support, on the other hand, almost always continues until the child is emancipated or reaches his or her majority.

Alimony is usually tax deductible by the person paying it; it must be declared by the person receiving it. Child support, on the other hand, usually is not deductible, nor is it added to the income of the person receiving it on behalf of the child. So: what will be paid? The balancing act is a delicate one: permanent (but deductible) alimony that counts as income versus terminable (but non-deductible) child support payments that do not.

As though things weren't confusing enough, the very definition of "alimony" is open to some dispute. The rules and regulations governing this point -- which is obviously of great importance from the point of view of individual tax planning -- are, unfortunately, changing constantly. Over the last few years, laws relating to taxation in divorce cases have changed. Because the patterns are still open to revision, however, your best move is probably to have your attorney look into the question. No advice could be offered in this book that would serve as a realistic substitute for consultation with a professional well-versed in the field.

As you might expect, the financial matters that accompany any divorce can become very complicated indeed. In addition to the alimony and child support aspects of the tax question, there's the issue of capital gains -- or, speaking more plainly, any gain that might be derived from the selling of assets during your divorce proceeding. Such assets could include a business, home, or any investments held jointly; even a transfer of an asset between the parties can have serious tax implications.

KEOUGH accounts, 401-K accounts, IRA accounts, and defined benefit accounts (as well as other types of tax savings acquired over the years) may result in different tax arrangements as a result of a divorce settlement. If the individual named in the account is not the only person to whom funds are distributed, the money involved may trigger a greater tax liability.

Bear in mind, too, that if a benefit plan to which you're entitled comes due to you during a divorce, the "money you've got coming" may be significantly less than you expect. You may have to pay immediate taxes, at a maximum rate, and the value of the plan could diminish tremendously. Your spouse, on the other hand, might acquire an asset of apparently equal value on which taxes have been deferred. It may seem as though your spouse has acquired "more," though each of you acquired the same number of pre-tax dollars in distribution.

Other questions that commonly arise during a divorce proceeding include the issues that surround the filing of an income tax return. Should a joint return be filed? *Can* one be filed? Should the finalization of a divorce be delayed so as to allow a joint return to be filed? Or should the divorce be expedited for tax reasons?

Consult with your accountant regarding the tax aspects of your case. He or she can be invaluable not only in resolving difficult questions such as these, but also in providing a second opinion on financial matters.

All the factors identified in this short review of tax questions in a divorce will differ from case to case. The correct course of action in your own individual case will depend on the income of the parties involved, the type and value of the distribution to be made, and numerous other factors. Unfortunately, it just doesn't pay to follow any "general rules" regarding taxes. There are no "general" divorce settlements. There's only your specific one.

Obviously, when it comes to dealing with the taxman, the word of your accountant and the abilities of your attorney are of the utmost importance.

ATTORNEY FEES

When discussing attorney fees, the standard arguments in a divorce situation sound something like this:

Why should I have to pay (his/her) attorney's fees? I've got my own to worry about!

Why shouldn't (he/she) pay my attorney's fees? Our side is the side that doesn't have the money; their side is loaded!

Funny thing is, both arguments are strong ones. That means you probably can expect some conflict on this issue -- whichever side you're on.

Usually, neither side is willing to try to understand the other side's problems concerning attorney fees. Remember that while the attorney may be a competent professional, he or she isn't necessarily your friend. Despite the fact that an attorney may be doing the best he can for his or her client, a strong likelihood exists that what's best for the attorney isn't being overlooked, either.

The best approach to negotiating this problem is a pretty simple one: *keep your attorneys "off the clock" and settle the issue between yourselves if at all possible --* preferably before you commit to working with a particular attorney. There are a lot of things that can consume your attorney's time (and, by extension, your money) in the divorce. This shouldn't be one of them. The fewer hours spent by an attorney in arguing and negotiating, the cheaper everything will be in the long run.

The parties involved might agree to pay both attorneys from a common fund. This fund could be raised from the sale of the house, one of the automobiles, or from a savings account. After coming to an agreement, the parties can advise their respective attorneys that they have reached an agreement between themselves regarding attorney fees, and that there is to be no further work on the matter. This will save time, effort, anxiety, and a *lot* of money.

Such difficulties, of course, may not arise in the first place if you've chosen the right lawyer. It goes without saying that you should, if possible, select an attorney who has been involved with matrimonial law for a number of years, is from your area, and is familiar with the local system.

It doesn't hurt if the attorney is honest, either. It can be a big help to have someone who can speak squarely with you in evaluating negotiations -- or evaluating the case before the negotiations start. If, for example, the attorney you initially select makes it clear to you that he or she does not like and cannot deal with the attorney picked by your spouse, you've been blessed with someone who is willing to share an important fact with you (a fact that probably means lower yearly income totals for the lawyer).

In that situation, you have a couple of options. You can ask your spouse to switch attorneys, or you can find another one yourself. Usually, the bottom line is that the party with the honest lawyer must (alas!) find someone else. It may not be fair, but it sure is economical. There's no sense paying for a lot of arguing you can see coming from a mile away.

Another step that's often overlooked is that of determining approximately how much your spouse is paying per hour for his or her attorney. If there is an hourly difference of, say, fifty dollars or more per hour (in either direction), something's probably wrong somewhere.

You'll have to make your own decision as to whether the attorneys involved are being overpaid or underpaid. If someone seems to have found a lawyer who is offering a "real deal," remember, you get what you pay for. Before either of you pays a retainer, set a consultation with the attorneys concerning fees. Ask why the rates appear to be adhering to separate standards. This could result in a reduction of fees by the higher priced attorney.

However you decide to go in paying attorney fees, try to reach an equitable agreement before the matter gets out of hand. Watching your attorneys argue for four or five hours will result in eight or ten very expensive, if entertaining, billable hours. Figure that you could be paying $125 an hour, and you might as well be making the down payment on a Lincoln Continental.

"GROUNDS FOR DIVORCE"

Before we leave the thorny subject of divorce, let's examine an issue of some confusion for many litigants: the question of grounds.

As a practical matter, the financial aspects of the case

are settled, in virtually all divorces, independent of the grounds for divorce. While you must have some grounds before the court will consider your divorce, from a realistic (i.e., monetary) standpoint, the grounds will have no bearing on the treatment your case receives. It is very likely that the whole question of grounds will, in the end, be nothing more than a technicality -- except, of course, where the emotions of the litigants are concerned. Though emotional issues are of no small import in such a divisive event as a divorce proceeding, the things you're paying your attorney to think about (child support, alimony, custody, property distribution) will almost always be resolved without any consideration being given to the grounds of the case.

Sound complicated? It really isn't. Every divorce begins with someone who seeks a divorce on some specific grounds. The question is, what are they?

Many states have implemented some form of "no-fault" divorce. What this means, basically, is that if you have been separated from your spouse for a certain period of time (regardless of the reason for the separation), and if there are no prospects for a reconciliation, either party can file for divorce on the basis of the length of the separation. The length of the separation itself constitutes the grounds.

A few states still require some type of "fault" indication on behalf of one of the parties when it comes to specifying grounds. Some categories of "faults" would include adultery, extreme cruelty, desertion, or other unpleasant occurrences, including that old favorite, irreconcilable differences.

This particular cause of action -- irreconcilable differences -- forms grounds that fall somewhere between the "no-fault" and "fault" approaches. If you are unable to use a separation as grounds, the irreconcilable differences approach is probably the most intelligent way to obtain a divorce.

All of this raises some unpleasant questions. Somebody -- one of the spouses -- has to file. Except in states where a joint complaint can be filed, somebody has to specify some grounds for dissolving the marriage if the divorce is to take place. In some instances, one spouse will feel quite strongly about taking the lead; in others, the issue will form the crux of a difficult problem.

Our suggestion is that you sit down with your spouse and discuss, adult to adult, the problems you have with one another. Try to determine between yourselves who will file and what the grounds will be. Try not to provoke conflict. Try not to aggravate any hard feelings that may exist between the two of you. This, again, is the kind of question that's best settled between you and your spouse, rather than the attorneys.

Such decisions require that each party exhibit responsible, adult approaches to the questions. Because of the emotions involved, this is sometimes hard to do. Each individual must be given the opportunity to discuss what he or she considers to be a problem. The other spouse may find it difficult to listen at this point, especially if the issue is a painful or difficult one that has been reviewed many times.

Sometimes the situation can be eased by the presence of a third party -- perhaps a clergyman or counselor, or even a mutual friend or trusted member of the family. To expedite this type of meeting and to keep it from dissolving into a battle, you may have to set up certain "ground rules." Each party, for instance, could be given a specified amount of time to state his or her case without fear of interruption. This approach can allow you to determine -- as amicably as possible -- what the grounds of divorce are going to be, with as little trauma as possible.

NOBODY WINS

Any divorce is an emotionally-charged situation for all concerned. This is the case not only for the litigants, of course, but also for the children, parents, relatives, and friends of the parties involved. Each spouse will feel, at times, that the other is being totally irrational and unreasonable. Often this impression will be justified. If the parties can try, nevertheless, to deal fairly with one another in the interests of a realistic, workable settlement, the questions that surround a divorce can be settled with a minimum of cost, anxiety, and frustration. If, on the other hand, each side is set on "teaching (him) (her) a lesson," there will be problems -- some that are long-term, some that are expensive, and some, sadly, that are both.

If the "best" divorce is a summit conference, with each side negotiating in good faith to determine a mutually agreeable set of guidelines in resolving a set of disputes, the "worst" divorce is a long-distance marathon. Don't trick yourself into believing you can (or should) try to "outlast" your "opponent."

CHAPTER TWELVE:
You Win!
You Lose!
What's Next?

YOU WIN!

The jury has just returned with a verdict in your favor. So what?

It's not over yet. Winning a judgment, as many a litigant has learned, is not the same thing as finalizing a judgment. Other potential obstacles remain, not the least of which is the less-than-thrilling prospect of encountering our legal system's appeals process.

Did you ever hear the joke about the lawyer who was asked by a reporter what he would do when justice prevailed in his case? The response was a simple -- but enlightening and very, very common -- one-word sentence: "Appeal."

The strategy that underlies an appeal is important to understand. The objective is not necessarily to win the case, but rather to exhaust the other side and/or force a more favorable settlement.

How is it done? The side that loses the case files a Notice of Appeal, usually with the Appellate Division of the Superior Court (or similarly designated court). Copies are served on your attorney, and on the judge who heard the initial case. Once this has been done, things tend to get quite boring.

In most jurisdictions, the appeals process is long, slow, and arduous. It is quite common for the time between the initial court determination and the *first* hearing at the *first* stage of an appeal to run between one and two years.

When an insurance company represents a defendant

on the losing end of a large judgment, the appeals process can be used as a tool to "convince" the opposition to settle the case for less than the amount awarded. Let's say you receive a judgment in the amount of $500,000, and the insurance company refuses to pay a penny until the appeals process is over. Although the money is in a bank somewhere earning interest, you do not have use of the funds until all the possible appeals are resolved. Throughout the process you face the possibility that the next court could overturn your previous victory. Bearing all this in mind, you might very well decide to settle for $400,000, despite the fact that the jury felt that you were entitled to $100,000 more. Chances are you'd recognize that $100,000 as a hypothetical figure, and think of the actual, honest-to-goodness cashable check for $400,000 as considerably more concrete.

Obviously, decisions concerning such large amounts of money should be made after detailed consultation with your attorney.

In the instances where a jury returns a verdict technically in favor of the plaintiff, but awards a sum of only $1.00, the defendant's insurance company may be willing to offer a substantially greater amount to settle the case before the appeals process even begins -- especially if the case is a highly publicized one. The carrier may be afraid that a far greater award will result on appeal. Of course, the best assessment of this type of case will be made by an experienced trial attorney, preferably the same one who has pursued the case through the initial stages. He or she will be familiar with all of the facts, and can advise you on the merits of settling out of court.

YOU LOSE!

The usual process of appeal followed by the loser of a case is, as outlined above, the filing of a Notice of Appeal. In addition, your side must order transcripts of the proceedings in the trial court. These transcripts are usually very expensive. Though rates can vary from region to region, expect to pay $100 for each hour spent in court. In other words, if there were five days of trial, and if court was in session seven hours a day, a reasonable estimate for a transcript of the proceedings would be approximately $3500.

That's not all. You'll have to make new payment arrangements with your attorney, which may entail new out-of-pocket costs; there are also filing fees to contend with in many jurisdictions, although these are usually modest.

Since you lost the original case, you may have lost some of your original confidence in your attorney as well, and could be tempted to find another. It is generally considered wiser, however, not to do so. Unless you're faced with gross incompetence or outright malice on the part of your attorney, think twice before obtaining new counsel. Think about how long it would take a new lawyer to attain the same familiarity with your case, to review all the transcripts, and to prepare a new case from scratch. Then think about paying for all that time. If you must find another lawyer, be sure to locate one who is knowledgeable in the field of law that encompasses your case.

Review all the factors -- particularly the additional costs involved -- before deciding to pursue an appeal. It is very possible that filing an appeal (even one which you stand a decent chance of winning) is financially unwise. Be sure to figure into your decision, too, the fact that delays of years, rather than months, are standard in the appeals process. You may "win" only in the sense that the previous trial is determined to have been unsound procedurally. That means you'll "get to" start all over again from square one in the same courthouse with a new trial date, a new set of attorney's fees to face, and the very real possibility that you'll lose twice in a row!

IF YOU DECIDE
TO APPEAL

You've examined all the relevant factors surrounding your case with your attorney. You want to appeal.

Assuming your side has done all the necessary paperwork, your first big step is...

Wait.

Sit around for, typically, two to four months and wait for the reporter to prepare the transcript of the original proceedings. Court reporters usually have huge backlogs. You can't do anything until the backlog is penetrated and your transcript is forwarded to you. So you must wait.

Months later, the transcript arrives. You're off and running (well, maybe walking briskly). Your attorney must now prepare a brief. This is a document setting forth what you believe to be the important facts in the case, and demonstrating that the original verdict was wrong. The goal is to receive a new chance to present your case.

There is no "typical" brief, but most run from thirty to sixty pages. Depending on the complexity of your case (and the ability of your attorney), you can expect to pay for anywhere between twenty and two hundred hours of work in preparing this document. The format, standards, and deadlines for composing and submitting briefs are determined within each jurisdiction.

By this time, you can expect to be thousands of dollars behind where you were at the time your trial ended. Your reward for all of this is that you get to allow your opponents -- known now as the "respondents" -- to file their brief, and then (you guessed it)...

Wait.

Anywhere from three to twenty months after you've reached this point, you get a notice of a hearing before the Appellate Court. This hearing takes place without a jury, and sometimes before more than one judge.

This is your lawyer's opportunity to argue your case -- and, of course, the opposition's opportunity to frame contrary positions. Don't expect any new testimony to be heard; these courts generally make determinations based on the arguments of the attorneys, the briefs filed, and the transcripts submitted.

Though the original trial may have taken many months, and the wait thereafter may have extended some years, the appellate hearing itself generally takes only a few hours. As we've seen, there are horrendous backlogs facing these judges, and their tendency is to focus on the "bottom line" factors of a case and dispose of the arguments in short order.

Your attorney will advise you of the date of the hearing, but, frankly, there's not much point in your attending.

You would be unable to gain any real clues as to the final outcome of your case, as judges give little or no indication in such settings of how they intend to rule. Unless you're interested in a civics lesson about the various procedural details of our country's appeals system, you're probably better off doing something more constructive and interesting, like reorganizing your sock drawer or going to a movie.

Once the hearing is over, you can, at long, long last, expect to...

Wait some more.

Any number of things can keep you in legal limbo. The attorneys may, for instance, be asked to submit additional arguments. More likely, they will be asked to sit around for one month to a full year more while the court makes up its mind about your case. Finally, assuming all the litigants are still alive and reasonably free from senility, the satisfaction of a decision from the Appellate Court can be relished to the fullest.

The decision may be in your favor; it may be in favor of your opponent; or it may be partially in your favor and partially in favor of your opponent. Of course, there also exists the distinct possibility that the Appellate Court may find that the trial court didn't do all it could have. In that case, there will be no new decision, the trial court will be asked to make further findings as to the facts of the case and everyone involved will get to...

Wait.

CHAPTER THIRTEEN: Defending Yourself... And Knowing When To Call A Lawyer

WHY LAWYERS HATE
TRAFFIC COURT,
SMALL CLAIMS COURT,
AND TENANCY COURT

After three years of law school, and perhaps several more years of practice, most lawyers are distinctly unenthusiastic about the prospect of entering the "pits" of our nation's legal system: traffic cases, D.W.I. (driving while intoxicated) matters, small claims disputes, and landlord-tenant conflicts.

Why? Aside from the generally low value associated with these cases, there is a compelling reason: there's very little room for "showing your stuff" in such legal disputes. The main goal of the judge is to get to the next case -- and to the hundreds of cases waiting beyond that one. It's a rare judge who will take the time required to consider each case in these areas as fully as it really demands.

Most traffic, small claims, and tenancy courts have a number of things in common. One common element is that they are all, for the most part, summary courts. A summary court is one which hears cases without a jury, and in which the judge must determine both the law and the facts. What this means is that the judge will decide what the possible facts are, and make decisions as to which version of the facts to believe, then apply the appropriate law to those facts. (By contrast, in a jury trial, the jury decides the facts and the judge decides the law.)

While it is generally inadvisable to argue your own case without a lawyer in a jury trial, doing so can sometimes be an economic and effective way of achieving justice in a summary trial like the ones we'll be examining in this chapter.

WHEN YOU SHOULD THINK ABOUT DEFENDING YOURSELF IN COURT

In all of the cases we'll be looking at in this chapter, you should follow a simple piece of advice before attempting to conduct your own case in front of a judge.

Invest in a short period of time with a good attorney to get a professional perspective on your case before determining that you are all you need to win the day.

Even if you decide to conduct your motor vehicle, small claims, or petty criminal case on your own, *you are not a lawyer.* Any intelligent attorney would take a pass on an offer to accept, without question, the duties and responsibilities of a total stranger who knows what it takes to get a certain job done. Think twice before trying to take on the duties and responsibilities of an attorney. Lawyers spend four years in college and three more in law school, and even then often learn only the most elementary aspects of their trade. You cannot master everything in a weekend.

Talk to a qualified attorney whose opinion you can

trust, and who will be honest enough with you to tell you when you can -- and can't -- take the money-saving step of representing yourself in court. At the very least, the attorney can give you an idea of the total potential value of the dispute, some estimate of the potential legal fees involved, and an understanding of the basic concepts surrounding your case. All too often, people defend themselves against the wrong claim or charge, and ignore or underplay the elements of their case that could admit a strong showing.

If you determine in your initial meeting that it would be unwise to represent yourself in a given case, secure appropriate counsel. You may wish to review the earlier sections of this book that outline the best ways to locate the right attorney for your case. If you cannot afford counsel, and are unable or unwilling to make use of a public defender, you can usually make an arrangement of some sort with your lawyer that will allow payments to be made over time.

THE KINDS OF CASES THAT PEOPLE WHO AREN'T LAWYERS CAN EXPECT TO WIN – AND WHAT THEY HAVE TO DO TO WIN THEM

Having consulted -- at least initially -- with an attorney, and determined that you wish to pursue your case independently, you may want to review the approaches taken in the cases in which a layman-as-advocate can expect to succeed.

As we've seen, the best setting you can ask for in representing yourself is probably the summary trial. Even in those cases in which you may have the right to a trial by a jury for a motor vehicle violation, you may waive that right if you wish to have the judge determine the outcome of your case instead. The procedures followed in this sort of waiver will vary from state to state.

Let's examine the most commonly successful types of cases that are self-litigated, and the types of approaches that work -- as well as those that don't. *Be sure to inquire as to the recent case law that surrounds the details of your case when you speak with your attorney* -- doing so will give you some idea of how effective the argument you plan on might be.

Speeding

What doesn't work:

My speedometer was broken.

My radar detector was broken.

I just put on new snow tires that go faster than I'm used to.

I haven't had a ticket in 55 years of driving.

What might:

I was driving the speed limit -- the officer who stopped me is incorrect, and was not aware of the actual speed limit. *Or:* The sign informing motorists of the speed limit could not have been seen by any motorist. (If the prosecutor fails to prove that the speed limit for the region in which you were stopped was what the arresting officer claims, you win. You may also have a very strong case if the sign can be demonstrated with photographs to be unfair, misleading, or impossible to make out.)

The device the officer used to time my rate of speed malfunctioned. (No matter what kind of instrument was used, it must usually be shown by the prosecutor to have been used accurately in this instance. Often, the prosecutor must provide proof that the officer was qualified to operate the device.)

Careless or reckless driving.

What doesn't work:

I sneezed.

I couldn't see oncoming traffic because the sun was in my eyes.

If there hadn't been ice on the road, I would have been able to avoid hitting anyone.

I was looking in the other direction.

(Remember that you are not being charged with *intentionally* driving in a dangerous manner, but rather with operating an auto without due care.)

What might:

The other driver was at fault. (Many police officers are instructed to issue tickets to all persons involved in an accident if there is any doubt whatsoever as to who was responsible. This is done to avoid confrontations at the accident scene, and to avoid involving an officer in "judgment calls" that he or she is unqualified to make. If you are involved in this type of case, a well-presented, fact-based, and rational defense can often be successful.)

The officer who issued the ticket did not see the accident, and is unqualified to assess who was or was not to blame. (This is factually correct in many, many accident cases.)

Small claims court (defendant)

What doesn't work:

We've never had any trouble like this before.

I didn't sell the customer the defective merchandise, an employee of mine did.

They're out to get me.

What might:

The merchandise was sold "as is." (Provide photographs of your place of business or other relevant information if there are signs posted or longstanding policies to this effect.)

I saw the product leave the store in the customer's

possession, and it was in perfect condition then. (If there is a witness who can corroborate this, ask him or her to testify for you.)

This product was not sold by our company, even though our company name appears on the item. (This will be most persuasive if you deal in items that are frequently sold second-hand at a later date. Of course, you can expect to lose the case after making this argument if you have in fact sold the customer the item and he or she can produce a receipt to prove it.)

This individual has no personal knowledge of the billing problems at issue, or of the services rendered or their quality, and is acting on second- and third-hand reports. (If the dispute concerns an overdue bill, and you are dealing with a functionary within the billing company, you may be able to establish that the individual in court with you would not know of payment if it had been made, for example, over the last few days.)

Small claims court (plaintiff)

What doesn't work:

He cheats all his customers.

I think I bought it there.

He lost a suit just like this last year.

What might:

Here's the ad that told me the product would perform in such-and-such a way; here's the product itself; here's my receipt. (Paperwork and supporting materials take on great importance in court. When in doubt, bring it with you.)

Here is the individual who handled billing problems arising out of our relationship with the defendant; her testimony should clarify any ambiguities.

(Personal appearances by key players in the conflict are time-consuming and difficult to schedule, but can make a big difference in the final outcome of the case.)

Tenancy court (tenant)

What doesn't work:

I lost my job four months ago.

I've always been a good tenant.

I'm pretty sure I paid that month, but I've misplaced my records.

What might:

The apartment is uninhabitable. (Provide ample evidence, photographic if at all possible, of the shortcomings of the rental unit. If you have made repeated efforts to arrange for repairs with the landlord, say so, and put forth any evidence that supports your claim.)

The check was delivered in the usual manner, but was never cashed by the landlord. *Or:* The landlord has apparently forgotten that I paid in cash that particular month. (These scenarios occur more frequently than you might imagine. Provide as much tangible proof of your claims as possible.)

Tenancy court (landlord)

What doesn't work:

They bring down the general quality of the neighborhood.

I don't care what the place looks like, what's crawling on the floors, or what's coming out of the faucets, they're behind two months.

I'm not sure where the building manager is, but I can answer any questions you want to ask -- except that one; and that one; and that one...

What might:

Here's the lease. Here are their signatures. Here's the building's supervisor. (Provide as much documentation as possible, being sure to ask all pertinent witnesses to accompany you to court. Many landlords show up for hearings alone and thereby create delays or losses that might otherwise have been avoided.)

A SPECIAL NOTE ON
TRAFFIC COURT ISSUES

Don't ever plead guilty to any traffic ticket without consulting a lawyer. The odds are that you'll discover that you should never plead guilty in a traffic court related matter without the court having entered a reservation that the plea cannot be used against you in any future civil case. If you plead guilty without that reservation, your guilty plea might be used against you as evidence in a later negligence trial. If you plead guilty *with* a reservation, the guilty plea cannot be used against you. If you plead *not* guilty, and are *found* guilty, the verdict generally cannot be used against you later on -- although it's possible that your testimony concerning the accident would be so used.

Obviously, each case is unique. Consult a lawyer for advice on how to handle your situation.

SOME TIPS ON
SURVIVING A SELF-
LITIGATED CASE

Listen carefully during the testimony to make sure that the requirements under the case law (which you can determine either from your initial consultation with a lawyer or through your own research) have been met. If they have not been met, *object* before any testimony is entered that will be damaging to your case. If you fail to object you may lose the opportunity to keep that testimony out of evidence. Object to any unfavorable statements attributed to someone other than the person giving testimony. This is usually considered hearsay, and will, with certain exceptions, be considered by the court to be unfair to you.

Ask questions during cross-examination; remember that this is not your turn to testify. Ask only questions that will help prove facts that support your case. Ask only questions to which you know the answer.

Demonstrate your points clearly and unemotionally during your own testimony. Prepare an outline of your version of events. Refer to it whenvever necessary. Do not attempt to improvise. Remember that your goal is not to win an argument, but to prove that you are making a legitimate claim -- of innocence, of due care, of right to compensation. Do not lie. You are under oath and have a legal obligation to tell the truth to the best of your ability.

MINOR NARCOTICS CASES

For many, the temptation exists to attempt a solo, attorneyless defense in minor narcotics cases or drunk driving incidents. It's usually a bad idea. If you can procure an attorney to help you with these legal problems, do so. A public defender is generally a sounder alternative than any attempt to manage such matters on your own.

In many states, minor narcotics offenses such as possession of small amounts of marijuana can be tried in a summary proceeding, though each state's approach will be unique. In addition, some states have decriminalized such possessions. What decriminalization means is often a matter of some confusion. It does not mean that you never need appear in court. It may simply mean that the class of offense has been declared by a state no longer to be considered a crime. In some states, you can still go to jail for a significant period of time -- usually up to six months.

Often, states that have decriminalized minor narcotics possessions have also instituted special programs targeted toward first time offenders or those guilty of comparatively minor infractions. These programs are generally designed to remove people from the criminal justice system who are not viewed as likely to commit subsequent violations, and require the completion of some fairly straightforward forms. In these instances, you may not require the assistance of an attorney to enter the program.

DRINKING AND DRIVING

In all but a very few states, a person accused of driving while intoxicated (D.W.I.) has the right to a trial by jury if he or she desires one. While the right may sometimes be waived in favor of a one-on-one encounter with a judge, it is advisable in this case as well to procure the advice of some sort of counsel rather than proceeding independently.

Virtually all states have what are known as "implied consent statutes." These laws, in effect, require that a person operating a motor vehicle submit to a physical test of some sort to determine the presence or absence of alcohol in the system. Breath tests (usually administered on a "breathalyzer" device) are most common. A refusal to submit to such testing either violates the statutes, or will result in administrative penalties (for instance, the loss of driving priviliges within that state).

Though each state can be expected to have standardized these test procedures, the fact remains that no such test is perfect. Here's what the prosecution must prove, either by testimony, evidence, or law, in most states in a contested D.W.I. case.

The testing device makes use of a valid scientific theory.

The device was functioning properly and accurately on the date of your test.

The operator of the testing device was qualified and licensed to operate the device.

The operator followed the correct procedures in this instance.

Nothing interfered with the test.

The device and operator complied with local and state requirements.

The prosecution may present an "observation" case -- in which witnesses testify to your behavior behind the wheel or your state of intoxication -- in order to supplement the test results. (In some instances, a prosecutor may rely solely on such testimony for conviction.)

Some motor vehicle and criminal offenses -- including drunk driving charges -- can have more severe (or "enhanced") penalties for repeat offenders. If you are facing a second or third drunk driving charge, it is imperative that you secure qualified counsel to represent you.

In order for the prosecution to seek (or the court to impose) enhanced penalties, the prior convictions must have been constitutionally imposed. If there was a constitutional problem in a prior conviction, such as failing to provide a lawyer to a person entitled to one, or neglecting to inform a defendant of his or her rights, the prior convictions can't be used as the basis for for enhanced penalties.

HOW NOT TO
DRINK AND DRIVE

All the above is quite interesting, but a little academic. After all, no one actually *plans* to be cited for drinking and driving! How can someone best avoid getting into that situation in the first place?

For starters, they can disregard most of the pocket

cards and charts on the market that purport to tell how much alcohol someone can consume without getting legally drunk. These guides usually assume that "a drink" is one ounce of, say, an 80 proof alcoholic beverage. But, as anyone who's ever been to a party knows, drinks can vary wildly in strength, and are often as high up on the scale as 150 proof. Drinks poured at home, or by an "amateur" bartender, can carry remarkable potency.

It is true that women *generally* have less ability to tolerate alcoholic beverages than men do, even when one is comparing similar builds. This is because of the different relative levels of water as a percentage of total body weight.

Alcohol usually takes between thirty and ninety minutes after consumption to enter the bloodstream. This means that, because you do not feel the effects of a drink as soon as you swallow it, you may feel perfectly sober when you start driving, but become steadily more intoxicated over time.

That same alcohol will dissipate at an *approximate* rate of somewhere between .01 and .015 percent of the blood count per hour. In other words, if you drink enough to cause a blood alcohol level of .20 percent, it will take *at least* six and one half hours to lose enough alcohol to get you below a .10 level again, and thirteen or fourteen hours to get you back to zero.

There are different legal and constitutional rights that may apply to drinking and driving charges -- each case can present different circumstances, and the statutes will vary from state to state. Obviously, the simplest, safest, and smartest way to approach the whole question is to avoid at all costs getting behind the wheel while there is even the slightest chance of your blood level exceeding legal limits.

CHAPTER FOURTEEN:
Money Matters --
Wills, Probate,
And Bankruptcy

WILLS

What can you do to prevent your intended heirs from becoming entangled in legal disputes over your estate after your death? It's a difficult question to confront, but one most of us should address.

If you do not prepare any will, you will be considered to have died "intestate" -- this means that the state assumes responsibility for the distribution of your assets. Because the courts involved must follow intricate (and confusing) laws on the subject, it is possible that your assets may be given to individuals to whom you did not intend to leave anything.

Accordingly, it is virtually *always* advisable to prepare a will; the question is, what kind of will should you prepare? A "do-it-yourself" will is known as a holographic will -- and, no, it has nothing to do with photographs. What a holographic will is (or, at any rate, probably should be) is last on your list of ways to dispose of property.

Law school textbooks feature many case studies of estates that have been sucked dry of their assets due to protracted legal wrangling over holographic wills. If you want your assets to go to your intended heirs -- and not to a bunch of lawyers you'll never meet -- don't take a chance on a holographic will. Those nameless lawyers can make life very difficult for those who try to collect and are challenged by miffed relatives not mentioned in the will.

What can they challenge? The legitimacy of your signature. Your mental capacity at the time the will was written. Your independence from undue influences at the time of writing and signing the will.

Remember that probate is the legal act of proving that a will is genuine. There's no reason to make that job difficult for your family, personal associates, or other beneficiaries.

Do it right. Hire an attorney to prepare your will. A simple will should cost somewhere between fifty and a hundred dollars, though an attorney will often spend considerably more time on the document than that figure would indicate. Why would an attorney "undercharge" you in this way? Most lawyers view drafting or executing a will as a necessary service to their clients, and usually out of professional courtesy, do not charge fees that reflect the actual billable hours involved. Of course, there is the possibility that a client will be impressed by such work, and will contact the lawyer if other legal questions or problems present themselves. In addition, many attorneys assume that the client's heirs will, if possible, contact the same attorney who wrote the will to handle other questions surrounding the estate's disposition.

When an attorney prepares your will, he or she will follow a set format that will anticipate potential difficulties after your death. The price incurred when you engage an attorney to draft your will is truly minimal when compared with the money your family may waste squabbling over your assets.

WHAT WILL – AND WON'T –
WORK IN A WILL

You may not be able to act with complete independence in framing your will; certain state statutes could interfere with your wishes. For instance, if you specifically exclude your spouse from receiving any of your property, he or she may be permitted to a certain percentage -- perhaps 33% of your estate -- regardless of your wishes.

Many people are surprised to learn that a will cannot provide for the distribution of all your assets. Unless your property is held by you and someone else as "tenants in common" (a topic we'll cover a little later in this chapter), you may have more limitations on the disposal of your property than you think. You may be unable to include in your will:

> The proceeds of an insurance policy where a named beneficiary appears.
>
> Property jointly held between you and your spouse.
>
> Property jointly held between you and some other person.
>
> Bank accounts designated as being the joint property of you and another person.
>
> Bank accounts and other assets held in trust for another person.
>
> Real estate jointly titled in your name and in the name of another person.
>
> Portions of real estate which, under the law of your state, belong to another person.

Surprised?

The law is very clear in most jurisdictions on the fact that the insurance company is obligated to pay the proceeds of a policy only to the person or persons named as beneficiary in the policy. A provision in the will attempting to modify the named beneficiary of an insurance policy is not effective.

In some instances, life insurance policies may be made payable to your estate; if this is the case, the proceeds will be paid as indicated in your will. Obviously, this is an action that should only be taken in conjunction with a qualified attorney or estate planner.

Real estate or personal property may be held jointly with another person. As a general principle of law, joint property is property that has what is known as a "survivorship interest." This means that, in the event of the death of one of the joint owners, all of the right to that property passes to the other joint owner. This is a point frequently misunderstood or misinterpreted.

Common problems arising out of this misunderstanding are, typically, those involving joint bank accounts. An older parent, unable to conduct affairs independently, might place a bank account in his name and the name of one of his children. What nobody realizes is that the bank signature card provides not only for the right of both parent and child to sign checks -- it also provides the joint owner (in this case, say, an eldest son) with prima facie ownership of the bank account after the parent's death. Nothing the parent can put in the will has any effect on the money in that account. Obviously, this can lead to hard feelings and awkward situations if the eldest son elects to retain all the assets lawfully his. (Of course, this type of case can be contested in court.)

The situation surrounding joint real estate holdings is similar. In circumstances where a husband and wife own property "by the entireties", or when individuals own land as "joint tenants with the right of survivorship", there are no halvsies. Neither of the parties can elect to pass on his or her "share" of the property in a will. Upon the death of one of the persons owning the property, the entire interest in the real estate belongs to the survivor.

Persons may also own real estate as "tenants in common" -- a partnership-type arrangement that clearly defines the interest of each party as exactly one-half of the real estate involved. Obviously, in this case, the person who dies *would* have the right to pass on his or her fractional interest in that real estate to beneficiaries designated in a will.

The question arises, however -- what happens if that beneficiary wants to sever his or her interests from that of the surviving "tenant in common"? This is frequently provided for by an appropriate insurance policy covering the value of the property, allowing the beneficiary to receive the cash value of the property without the original "partner" having to sell the real estate itself. Of course, this all must be planned out well ahead of time with the benefit of qualified professional advice. (By the way, the same principle would work in distributing any partnership interest, including an interest in an operating business.)

Finally, in the area of trusts, there are also limitations on what may or may not be bequeathed in a will. Let's examine the situation in which a person who dies while a property remains in trust makes "adjustments" in preparing his or her will. In a lifetime trust, the person writing the will has already created an interest in the beneficiaries of the trust. These "specifications" cannot be changed by any provision of the will. A common example of this situation is the so-called "Totten Trust". In this scenario, a parent might open a bank account in her own name "in trust for my child John" -- and upon the death of the mother, accordingly, the trust operates to provide that the money in the account goes to John regardless of any provisions in the mother's will.

PLANNING AHEAD

As you can see, there are many potential problems that can accompany determining the disposition of your estate. That's why it's an excellent idea to make your plans well in advance; this will allow you to resolve, early on, any difficulties your family may encounter later.

Of course, early preparation of your will permits you to choose the persons to whom you wish property to go and the items and amounts you want them to have. It also enables you to designate the executor, the person who will administer the assets of your estate. That person will collect your assets, pay the necessary expenses and taxes, and then distribute the balance to your designated beneficiaries in accordance with the provisions of the will.

PROBATE:
TRUSTS, TAXES
AND WILLS

A great deal has been written on the subject of avoiding probate -- in other words, limiting inheritance and estate taxes by not having the title to property pass at the time of death, or limiting or reducing the amount of property that is so delivered. While this approach may be desirable when substantial estates are in question, avoiding probate is not for everyone. Let's examine the pros and cons of this briefly -- recognizing, of course, that such matters as establishing lifetime trusts for the purpose of limiting future tax liability should not be decided without obtaining qualified professional advice.

You can create a trust that will set aside certain assets to the custody of a trustee, providing that income from that trust is paid to you over your lifetime. The principal remaining in that trust can, at the time of your death, be paid to designated heirs. If the trust is revocable, no savings on death taxes will pass on to your heirs. The reason: you would have had the power to remove the assets from the trust during your life.

By the same token, if you decide on an irrevocable trust in order to qualify for a tax benefit, you will be unable to use any of the assets in the trust during your lifetime. Clearly, this is a serious step. You should have an adequate estate in your own name before contemplating the creation of such a trust.

Creating a trust in your will may not lessen estate taxes at the time of your death, but can save your children -- and perhaps your grandchildren as well -- on such taxes over time. There are certain ways to create trusts by will, for instance, that allow the surviving spouse the benefit of the income of the trust money until his or her death, at which time the principal passes to the children or grandchildren. In effect, this kind of trust avoids submitting the same property to inheritance and related taxes on two separate occasions.

Another advantage to setting up a trust in your will may be the discretion afforded in passing on funds to young adults. Most jurisdictions will allow a child to receive a substantial amount of money at the age of eighteen. If you wish more time to pass before the funds are distributed, you can specify this in your will. You may also provide that the trust money be used for a specific purpose, such as education.

BANKRUPTCY --
WHAT IS IT?

Bankruptcy is really nothing more or less than the prioritization of manageable debt -- and the elimination of unmanageable debt problems.

Before making a final decision as to whether or not you should file for bankruptcy, consult with an attorney. Bankruptcy is one of those areas of our law in which it is absolutely essential to locate a specialist in the field. Try to find a lawyer who works exclusively, or almost exclusively, in bankruptcy matters.

Two or three trips to bankruptcy court will help you identify a number of lawyers experienced in the field. Like many other specialties, this one is prone to certain nuances and an almost "clubby" atmosphere in the courtroom. Try to select the most accomplished and effective attorney. Once you learn the names of the lawyers, it is a simple matter to find them in the phonebook and call for an appointment.

Your main question during the first interview, of course, is that of determining whether or not bankruptcy is worth pursuing. Bring with you a list of your assets, including personal property. Make sure you also have a list of all your debts, including your electric bill, phone bill, mortgage balance; and other items. It might be a good idea to summarize all this information in a chart form for your attorney's use.

Basically, there are two types of bankruptcy available to most individuals: Chapter Thirteen and Chapter Seven.

A third type, Chapter Eleven, is used primarily by businesses. The filing fees are higher, and the process incorporates the restructuring of debts, rather than their liquidation.

BANKRUPTCY:
CHAPTER THIRTEEN

Under Chapter Thirteen, a trustee is appointed by the federal court to review your assets and debts. Your attorney suggests to the court a plan for the payment of all the creditors over a period of time not to exceed five years. A bankruptcy judge then approves or disapproves of the plan, and payments are made based on your assets -- including the equity in your home or other assets, and based on your continuing income.

If you do not have the income to pay all of the debts that are owed, you may be permitted to pay the amount of non-exempt equity in your home or other assets in monthly installments over the same period of time. When this amount has been paid, all of your debts are considered to have been satisfied.

To be eligible for this type of bankruptcy, you must meet certain requirements. You must be a wage-earner, a professional with a regular income, or a small business owner. You must not have unsecured debts over $100,000. You must not have secured debts over $350,000. (This type of debt is secured by some pledge of personal property.)

Once you file, there are distinct restrictions placed on your creditors. All suits against you for nonpayment of bills, whether new or presently pending, must be stopped upon notice. In addition, anyone who is owed money by you is precluded from writing to you or telephoning you in an attempt to collect. Creditors cannot contact your employer in any manner; your wage cannot be garnished (withheld). If you do have a garnishment against your wages, it will terminate.

Your employer must pay your full salary without any deductions for your creditors. All service charges, late charges, and interest charges are discontinued, and creditors cannot repossess or seize property you've used as collateral without permission from the court. Collection attempts against anyone who has co-signed for you on any of your debts must, at least temporarily, stop.

BANKRUPTCY:
CHAPTER SEVEN

The other type of bankruptcy, Chapter Seven, is the most widely known method that allows you, in effect, to wipe out all of your dischargeable debts and begin your economic life all over again. This type of bankruptcy can be entered into at any time without restriction on the amount of the debt. Chapter Seven bankruptcies can be filed only once every six years.

One widespread but incorrect belief about Chapter Seven is the idea that you not only wipe out all your debts, but also must part with all of your assets. The truth of the matter is that there are specific exemptions on assets that you may retain, regardless of the amount of debt you owe.

Some states will allow greater exemptions than others. See an attorney to get the specifics in your state. The list provided below will give you a good idea of what you might expect.

You can probably keep...

One motor vehicle with a total equity value of up to $1,200; your household or personal property up to a value of $4,000; jewelry up to a value of $500; professional books or tools of the trade up to $750; cash value of insurance policies up to $4,000; professionally prescribed health aids without limit; your home or property with a value up to $7,500 (if you do no have a home, you can usually allocate up to $3,750 to personal property, provided no single item is worth more than $400).

In addition, you can expect to be allowed to have additional property such as tax refunds and savings accounts with a value of up to $400.

If you are filing for bankruptcy with your spouse, you can double all the amounts given above.

Chapter Seven, as you can see, does not leave you high and dry. It leaves you, instead, with all (or most) of your clothing, a car, some money in your pocket, and a good measure of self-respect. Remember that bankruptcy, in this day and age, no longer carries the stigma it once did.

SOME BANKRUPTCY
WARNINGS

Don't forget to consult a qualified bankruptcy attorney.

Don't go on a shopping spree prior to filing for bankruptcy in the hope of having the resulting debts discharged by the court. There are restrictions on last-minute purchases; consult with your attorney about specifics.

Don't expect to have your taxes, alimony or child support payments, or debts incurred fraudulently discharged during a bankruptcy proceeding. These bills will have to be paid no matter the outcome of your action in court.

Don't be overly concerned about your ability to pay your attorney; filing for bankruptcy is not usually all that expensive. The real difficulty usually is one of locating the right lawyer.

Don't rush a decision to file. You might want to consider contacting all of your creditors by letter, advising them that you anticipate filing for bankruptcy, and inquiring as to the possibility of compromising on the amount you owe in order to wipe out the debt. If you are uncomfortable doing this, or wish to add impact to your communication, you might ask your attorney to send the letter out under his or her signature. Be sure that you are in a position to settle the debts (on a smaller scale, of course) if you follow this procedure.

CHAPTER FIFTEEN:
The Last Word

THE END...?

The law is a constantly-changing thing. Principles shift, new theories emerge, precedents are challenged.

From the layman's point of view, however, one suggestion remains valid year after year.

If it's at all possible, stay out of court. That's the advice with which we began this book, and that's how we're ending it, as well. Of course, you're no doubt aware by now that there are many, many situations in which you have no choice but to become a participant in our legal system. With this book, however, we hope to have offered enough information on the "inner workings" of that system to allow you to make some informed decisions relative to your legal strategy. With the help of a qualified attorney, your options should be realistic ones, and your position, in or out of court, should be less likely to be damaged by hasty reactions, ill-conceived objectives, or misinformation.

Shakespeare wrote, "Beware of entrance to a quarrel -- but being in, bear't that the opposed may be beware of thee." The law and the world in which it operates may change, but even after over three hundred fifty years, it's nice to know that some advice remains dependable. It's with the Bard's own counsel that we close the main section of this book.

Good luck!

APPENDIX

LEGALESE-TO-ENGLISH GLOSSARY

The purpose of this section is not to provide a definition of every term your lawyer may use, or to clarify for you every legal term that may arise in your case. Rather, our intention is to provide the meanings of key words with which you should be familiar before going to court, and to give you an idea of the practical use to which such phrases are put. Study this glossary, but bear in mind that it is no substitute for consultation with your attorney about confusing or contradictory aspects of your case.

A.G.   This is slang for any Attorney General. It also can refer to any assistants on his or her staff.

Acquittal.   This is used in criminal law, and is a verdict indicating that the State has not been able to prove guilt beyond a reasonable doubt. An acquittal does not mean that a person was proved innocent, only that the State failed to prove its case with sufficient clarity to win conviction.

Additur.   In this instance, a plaintiff gets a low jury award; the judge determines that a greater monetary award than the one determined by the jury is deserved, and orders that a new trial on damages begin -- unless the terms he or she specifies are accepted.

Adjournment.   This is what happens when your case is

postponed for some reason.

Adultery. The term refers to a married person who has an affair. An unmarried person cannot commit adultery.

Advocate. Another word for attorney.

Affidavit. Signed in the presence of a notary public or an attorney, this is a document containing statements made by you which you swear are true.

Agent. You're generally responsible for this person's actions on your behalf; he or she works for you at your request.

Alimony. In order for an ex-spouse to to continue living in the style to which he or she has become accustomed, these payments are made.

Appeal. This is what you take to a higher court, either because you lost or because you didn't get everything you wanted.

Appellate Court. This is the court that hears your appeal.

Arraignment. Although most citizens are broadly familiar with the rights associated with the *Miranda* decision, an accused person must still be formally notified of them at a short hearing, and must be informed at that hearing of the charges against him or her. This hearing is known as an arraignment.

Arrest. This is when the police will not allow you to move out of their sight. You do not have to be taken to a police station to be under arrest. You do not have to be told that you are under arrest to be under arrest.

Assault. This occurs when a person creates in someone's mind a reasonable apprehension of immediate harm or offensive contact. See also *Battery.*

Attorney at law. The term describes someone licensed by a state to practice law.

Attorney General. This person is the highest ranking law enforcement officer in a state or federal government.

Bail. This is an amount of money that must be paid to obtain release before trial by a defendant. Bail is often required in disorderly persons offenses as well as more serious criminal matters.

Bailment. A contract for bailment exists when a person turns over a piece of property for safekeeping or a similar purpose, with the understanding that the item will be returned or satisfactorily handled. For example, when you leave your clothes with a dry cleaner, you are the bailor; the dry cleaning establishment is the bailee.

Battery. This term refers to the actual touching that occurs during an assault.

Brief. This is a written presentation of the law and facts of your case.

Burden of proof. This is a term used to indicate what the parties must prove and who has to prove it. A plaintiff has the burden of proving a defendant's negligence; a defendant must prove the plaintiff's contributory negligence. In civil cases, the burden of proof is usually a preponderance of the believable evidence; in criminal cases, the State (which always has the burden of proof) must overcome the defendant's presumption of innocence by proving guilt beyond a reasonable doubt.

Challenge. This is what the attorney does when a juror is unacceptable and should be excused before a trial begins. There are two kinds of challenges -- "peremptory" ("I don't have to give you any reason at all, Your Honor") and "for cause" ("I submit that this juror is inappropriate because he is the defendant's brother").

Charge. A judge makes this statement to jurors at the end of the presentation of a case to inform them of what the law is before they enter into deliberations.

Circumstantial evidence. As distinguished from direct evidence -- that which a witness sees, feels, hears, tastes, or touches -- this is evidence based on deduction and inference.

Civil. Basically, this term applies to anything that is not criminal -- that is, anything that can't land you in jail, result in a fine, or put you on probation.

Closing statement. This is an attorney's final address to the jury. Usually the plaintiff's side goes last in a civil case. In a criminal case, the State will go last.

Contingency fee. Under this arrangement, if the attorney doesn't win any money with your case, he or she doesn't get paid. If the attorney does get a recovery, he or she gets a certain percentage of your award or settlement.

Corpus delecti. In a criminal case this term might refer to a dead body.

Counsellor at law. This is another term for attorney.

Costs. This refers to the amount of money needed to file a complaint, effect service on the defendant (or third-party defendant), and execute related tasks.

Comparative negligence. The idea is similar to that of contributory negligence (see below). In some states, a plaintiff can recover from the defendant, as long as the plaintiff is not more than 50% negligent. If the plaintiff is 51% negligent, he or she cannot recover. If the plaintiff is 50% negligent, he or she can recover 50% of what is determined to be the total damages arising out of the case.

Contributory negligence. In a civil action, this is what a defendant will claim that the plaintiff bringing the action exhibited. The claim is usually that the plaintiff failed to exercise the necessary reasonable care for his or her own safety. While the plaintiff has the burden of proving the defendant's negligence, the defendant has the burden of proving the plaintiff's contributory negligence.

"The Court." This is another term for the judge in the case.

Court clerk. Typically, the court clerk, during the trial, marks the exhibits for identification (and into evidence), swears in the jury, and takes the jury's verdict in front of the judge, the attorneys, and the litigants.

Court reporter. This is the person who takes down, verbatim, everything that occurs before the court.

Criminal. The word applies to things you can go to jail for, be put on probation for, or be fined for -- in short, that which is not civil.

Cross-examination. This occurs when the other side gets an opportunity to ask you and your witnesses questions. Leading questions (see the section on courtroom objections) are permitted during cross-examination.

Damages. Usually, this refers to the pain and suffering a person was forced to undergo, the amount of money a person actually lost, or the value of property that was damaged.

Defendant. If you are sued or charged with a crime, disorderly persons offense, or a traffic violation, you are the defendant.

Demand for jury. This comes at the end of the complaint. Usually, if you fail to make a demand for jury, you won't get one. If you want a jury, your lawyer must make sure your complaint or answer says so.

Depositions. The other side asks out-of-court, oral questions regarding the incident in question. Your answers must be factual.

Direct examination. This is the opposite of cross-examination; your attorney tries to establish your case -- either through asking you questions or asking your witnesses questions.

Discovery. The term refers to the portion of the case that includes interrogatories, depositions, and the gathering of basic information. Every case incorporates the process. In some cases, there's quite a lot of discovery - in others, there's very little. If there's very little, it may means one of two things: either you have a good lawyer who knows what's necessary to win and is doing no more than that in order to save you money; or you have a bad lawyer who simply isn't doing the job.

Evidence. This generally encompasses anything that leads to a conclusion that either the plaintiff or the defendant is right about a given situation.

Ex parte. This is the situation in which you're allowed to come into court *without notifying the other side* of anything until what you're looking for from the court is obtained. Such a situation leads to the issuing of an order by the judge, which usually surprises the other side.

Expert witnesses. These are people who have credentials sufficient to justify testifying about a certain technical or specialized area -- and who are not expected to have had direct sensory experience of the conflict being reviewed.

Filing. The state court system will select an office as the designated location to which you should direct the documents you file such as your complaint or answer.

Grand jury. More than twelve persons sit on this jury, which decides whether or not an individual should be indicted for the alleged commission of a crime.

Identification. This must be done in every criminal case in order to sustain a criminal conviction. Identification constitutes one of the most important reasons for you to secure representation by an attorney; on your own, you'll probably be pigeonholed as "the defendant," whether or not you are a victim of mistaken identity. A good lawyer can help you effectively contest the charge that you're "the one who did it."

In camera. This refers to what takes place in a judge's chambers. Sometimes lawyers will put statements on the record in this environment. A court reporter will record the statements.

In court. Certain things must happen within the physical confines of the courtroom -- identification of the defendant, for instance.

Incompetent. The term describes someone the court feels is unable to handle his or her own affairs (for instance, an infant). It can also refer to a witness's inability to testify to an event, idea, or observation.

Indemnification. In a civil suit, such as a negligence or product liability dispute, Defendant A may demand indemnification from Defendant B on the theory that B is entirely responsible for any judgment that may be entered against A.

Indictable. When you have "an indictable" against you, it's time to get an attorney if you don't already have one. The phrase describes the indictment that accuses you of a crime -- in most jurisdictions, one which entails at least six months in jail upon conviction.

Indictment. This is the actual piece of paper that informs you of the crime the state says you committed. Again, if you get one of these, find a good lawyer.

Injunction. The court tells you you can't do something you either have been doing or intend to do. If you fail to comply with an injunction, you may be committing a criminal act.

Interrogatories. Written questions that often serve as the initial step in discovery are known by this name. They can be served on any party to a civil lawsuit.

Intervening cause. This is an act of an independent person or entity which destroys the cause-and-effect connection between a defendant's negligent act and a plaintiff's injury. If a defendant can show that the accident was initiated by an intervening cause, he can often escape liability to the plaintiff.

Invitee. In negligence cases, this is an individual who is permitted to enter or remain on a person's property for the owner's or occupier's own purposes. When you enter a store or shop to browse, you are considered an invitee.

Judgment. When a judge or jury says you owe someone a certain amount of money, a judgment is rendered against you in that amount.

Judicial notice. A judge may take judicial notice of certain facts -- in other words, designate them as being so generally known or of such common acceptance that no proof is necessary to confirm them.

Jurisdiction. This describes the contact you may or may not have with a specific court. If you are a resident of the state of California and have never had anything to do with New York, it is unlikely that the New York state courts have jurisdiction over any of your legal problems.

Jury. This body is the entity that makes the decision about your case. Juries can vary in number and may be substituted by a judge in some instances.

Jury list. Your attorney will be given a list that will supply information about prospective jurors in your case. This list will provide names, addresses, and (usually) occupations.

Jury verdict. The term refers to any determination by the jury.

Lawyer. The term describes someone licensed by a state to practice law.

Lessor. This means a landlord.

Lessee. This refers to someone who rents a piece of property from someone else.

Lien. This stands on the records against your real estate or other property. It prevents you from transferring or selling the property until the lien itself (a certain sum of money) is paid.

Licensee. In negligence cases, this is a person who, by inference, is permitted to enter or remain upon land or property with the consent of the owner or possessor of that land (for instance, a door-to-door salesman).

Litigants. The parties to any action are called the litigants. A litigant can be a plaintiff, defendant, third-party defendant, fourth-party defendant, fifth-party defendant...

Local rules. These usually apply to the Federal courts, but can apply to state courts as well. Different courts have different rules that apply to different types of cases.

Malingering. Lawyers, judges, doctors, and insurance company representatives use this phrase to describe those individuals who are allegedly faking an injury or exaggerating its severity.

Medical malpractice. This is a very specialized type of law which concerns itself with cases where it's claimed that a hospital, a doctor, or other medical worker has erred in diagnosing or treating a patient. Plaintiffs' attorneys often refer to this type of litigation as "medical negligence" on the theory that the term "malpractice" can offend jurors.

Miranda warnings. If you are arrested, you must be advised of: your right to remain silent; the fact that anything you say can and will be used against you; your right to consult with an attorney prior to and during any police interrogation; the fact that an attorney will be engaged for you if you can't afford one; and your right to stop a conversation and ask for an attorney if you do decide to speak with the police on your own. The rights were first standardized in the famous *Miranda vs. Arizona* case.

Mistrial. A court can declare a mistrial when something occurs during the trial which substantially affects the right of one (or perhaps both) of the parties to receive a fair trial. A mistrial can also occur when a jury is unable to reach a verdict. When a mistrial is declared, the jury is disbanded, and the trial begins again before another jury.

Motions. These are requests for the issuance of an order granting you something to which your side believes you're entitled. Most can be brought in both civil and criminal cases.

Negligence.   In civil cases, this means the failure to exercise a reasonable degree of care for the safety of others. It may mean performing an act which a "reasonable person   of ordinary prudence" would not have done; it may mean the failure to do what such a person would otherwise have been sure to do.

Nolo contendere.   This is a plea in a criminal case by a defendant.   The individual is subject to conviction, but does not acknowledge guilt.   See *Pleas*.

Notice to produce.   This list of items, which comprises all the things the other side wants you to show up with, is usually quite extensive.

Objection.   A lawyer makes one of these when the other side: asks what appears to be an improper question; makes an apparently improper statement; or attempts to introduce physical evidence in what seems to be an improper manner.

Open court.   When the proceedings may be observed by the public, this is how the courtroom environment is described.

Opening statement.   In civil and in criminal cases, each lawyer has the opportunity to make a preliminary statement to the judge or jury concerning what that attorney hopes to prove or disprove.

Opinions.   When a judge gives his or her oral or written decision concerning a case's outcome, he or she renders an opinion.

Orders.   Any determination by the court before judgment is called an order.

P.D.   This is slang for Public Defender.

Parties.   See **Litigants.**

Per se.   "The word I just used   speaks for itself.   No further proof is necessary."

Perjury.   Lying while under oath is frowned on by all judges.   It's illegal, and people do get sent to jail for it. Don't let the judge send a message to future perjurers by incarcerating you.   Tell the truth.

Petit jury.   The term is another way of referring to the jury that will make a determination in the case -- as opposed to the grand jury, which decides on whether or not someone should be indicted.

Plaintiff.   This is the person who is complaining that something wrong was done to him or her.   The plaintiff presents his or her proofs first.

Pleas.   This is the presentation by the defendant at the outset of the trial: guilty, not guilty, innocent, or nolo contendere (Latin for "I do not wish to contend"). Sometimes people will fail to enter any plea; in these cases, the court will usually enter a not guilty plea.

Polling the jury.   You've lost your case.   You want to query the jury personally about the result.   The judge asks each juror if the vote recorded was indeed cast.

Probate.   This is what is done to a Last Will after a person dies.

Proof of service.   This is an affidavit, usually submitted by the sheriff or similar official, showing that certain paperwork has been sent to the appropriate parties.

Proximate cause. The court will tell a jury that a proximate cause is a cause which naturally and probably led to produce a certain result -- for instance, an accident.

Reasonable doubt. In a criminal case, the prosecution must prove, beyond a reasonable doubt, that the defendant is guilty. What is a reasonable doubt? That which will not allow a jury to say that the defendant acted as claimed by the prosecution. If the State fails to prove -- to all twelve jurors -- a case beyond a reasonable doubt, the criminal matter's defendant, who is presumed innocent, must be acquitted.

Reasonable man. This is the standard that is used in negligence cases. All conduct is judged by what a reasonable man, not an extraordinary man, of ordinary prudence, would do under circumstances the same as or similar to those in the lawsuit. A reasonable man also, of course, refers to a reasonable woman.

Res ipsa loquitor. In an ordinary negligence case, the mere fact that an accident occurred does not indicate that the defendant was negligent. In some instances, however, an accident's very occurrence may, in and of itself, be sufficient proof of negligence. Under those circumstances, the doctrine of *res ipsa loquitor* applies.

Remand. The Appellate Court thinks the court that heard the original case made an error. The case is sent back to the trial court to be heard again.

Remittur. If the the judge feels the plaintiff has gotten too much money from the jury, the judge can take actions that will reduce the award. The amount taken away is the remittur. See *Additur.*

Request to charge. This is what each lawyer asks the judge to tell the jury about the law they must use to decide the case.

Rules. These govern procedures in court.

Rules of evidence. The term refers to guidelines about what is or is not admissible in court, as well as what it takes for something to be admissible as evidence.

Sanctions. This is what the court can do to you if you don't comply with its order -- i.e., put you in jail, fine you, and so forth.

Search warrant. This is what the police must usually have before they can enter your house without permission.

Sequestration. This excludes people in court from hearing what certain witnesses have to say.

Service. Papers (e.g., a subpoena) are officially handed over in person to someone.

State. The State's case is that of the county, town, state, or even the Federal government prosecuting "the people's" case.

Statute of limitations. Each state has a statute specifying the time period after a given event that a legal action may be initiated concerning it. In many states, for example, an automobile accident victim must institute suit within two years of the accident date or forfeit any chance of recovering against the defendant.

Strict liability in tort. This means that a manufacturer, seller, or supplier has an obligation to ensure that its product is reasonably safe for use in its intended and reasonably foreseeable purpose. The term is used in product liability litigation.

Subpoena. Once you receive this document requiring you to appear in court, be sure to comply fully with all its instructions. The judge may order your arrest in order to get you to appear.

Summary judgment. This is issued when you're involved in a civil case and there's no question as to the liability of the other side. Your attorney can submit a motion for summary judgment to the judge, who can make a determination that no important facts are in dispute. If the judge makes that determination, he or she then rules on the issue of liability.

Summons. This is a document you receive at the same time as a complaint. It tells you how many days you have to answer the complaint and where to send your answer.

Superseding cause. See *intervening cause.*

Supreme Court. There are Supreme Courts in each state (which go by a number of names); there's also one Supreme Court of the United States. The Supreme Court is the court of last resort.

Transcript. When testimony is taken in court or during a deposition, the court stenographer transcribes the testimony into a booklet form. Transcripts are expensive to order, and are billed at a set rate per page.

Trespasser. If you enter or remain on another person's land or property without a privilege to do so, you're trespassing. Normally, an owner or occupier of land does not owe any duty to a trespasser, other than to keep from intentionally injuring that trespasser. (In other words, it's difficult for a trespasser to win a suit for negligence against the person whose property has been trespassed.)

Venue. The term describes the appropriate place to bring a suit. Usually, the venue will refer to the place where one of the parties resided or had a place of business, where an accident occurred, or where a contract was signed.

Wade hearing. The name arises from the *United States vs. Wade* case. In criminal cases, this takes place out of the presence of the jury, when a defendant contests the validity of his or her out-of-court identification. During the hearing, the court must be convinced that the out-of-court identification was not tainted by unconstitutional methods. If the out-of-court identification is invalid, it cannot be presented to the jury, and the prosecution must link the defendant to the crime by other means.

Workers compensation court. In many states, if you're injured on the job, you have the right to recover from your employer or his insurer a sum based on the percentage of your disability. The recovery is permitted even when your employer was not responsible for your injury -- and even if your conduct was the sole cause for that injury. In order to obtain the money, you must file a petition with the workers compensation court in your jurisdiction.

A CHECKLIST OF
COURTROOM OBJECTIONS

Objections to the questions that are posed in a courtroom are, generally, a subject taught only in law school advocacy courses. For the experienced practitioner, these objections are a matter of instinct. For the new and inexperienced trial attorney, they're a maze of misunderstood and often-misstated technical terms. For the client, they are, for the most part, gibberish.

Here's a brief accounting of the underlying principles of the major objections you're likely to hear posed in your case. They are given in (roughly) descending order of popularity.

Leading question. Technically, this is a question that suggests to the witness an answer desired by the examiner. It's often assumed that all leading questions are ones which require a yes-or-no answer, while questions that begin with such phrases as "Would you please state for us whether or not..." aren't. Neither assumption is always correct in every instance.

The distinction between a leading and an acceptable question turns on the issue of whether or not an ordinary man would get the idea that the examiner wished one response rather than another.

Determining the suitability of such questions is entirely up to the judge. A court's discretion in allowing or failing to allow questions one side claims are leading is virtually never challenged, unless the decision contributes somehow to a denial of due process.

Irrelevant and/or immaterial. This means that the questions call for an answer that has no evidential value. Such a claim, of course, is likely to be open to dispute from the examining side -- otherwise the question would not have been posed in the first place. Strictly speaking, a question is relevant and material if the evidence to be garnered by it may tend to prove a fact which bears in any manner on a question or circumstance in the dispute.

Asked and answered. The claim here is that a question has already been posed that covers the same subject as the present question, and that the response is already in evidence.

Once again, this type of determination by the judge is discretionary. A judge may allow such a question, for instance, if the prior response was vague, or if there is a question about separate versions of the same event from one witness.

Speculative (and/or: Calls for a conclusion). The idea is that the witness is being asked to render opinion-based testimony which he or she is not competent to render. This objection can also incorporate the claim that the witness is testifying concerning facts he or she did not personally experience.

As we learned in an earlier chapter, opinions on the

ultimate issue of a case are generally not allowed from lay witnesses. However, opinions may sometimes be admitted when a proper foundation has been laid. For instance, an attorney might inquire of a lay witness how fast she thought she was driving at the time of an accident.

With a foundation of questions set up to include important facts (i.e., that the witness had looked at the speedometer five minutes before the accident and had seen a reading of fifty-five miles per hour; that she had not stepped on the brake until the accident itself) a judge could be expected to allow such a witness to make an estimate of her speed, even without a work background as a physicist or police officer.

Improper question. This encompasses a number of objections. Among the most liekly candidates: a compound query that asks two or more questions at the same time; an ambiguous question in which one or more words are open to multiple interpretations; or a question that assumes a fact not in evidence ("When did you stop beating your wife?").

Argumentative. Though a certain amount of leeway can be expected during cross-examination, as a general rule it is not permissible for an examiner to argue with or badger a witness. This objection usually surfaces when a series of questions has failed to elicit any new facts, and when continued questioning serves only to challenge a witness.

Privilege. This objection is used when the examiner's question might violate some basic privilege of the witness: physician/patient, husband/wife, lawyer/client, etcetera. Of course, rulings on this matter will depend on the standards that exist in the particular state.

Hearsay. To simplify matters perhaps a step too far, hearsay is second-hand testimony that is unacceptable as evidence in a case ("This guy I know at work said he saw the guy steal the car"). However, hearsay probably is the objection most often made erroneously. Many lawyers are unsure of what does and does not constitute hearsay in testimony.

All statements made out of court -- and subsequently reported by another witness for the truth of the matter in question -- may be considered hearsay, but numerous exceptions exist, and many out of court statements are admissible.

Occasionally lawyers will object to what sounds to them like hearsay, but isn't. If the objective is not to determine the central facts in the dispute, but only to ascertain whether or not a certain statement was made ("Mr. Brown told me it was safe to go into the mineshaft, yes sir"), then the testimony is not hearsay.

No foundation. This is an objection generally used when a lawyer wishes to challenge a witness' credentials or mastery of the facts. The idea is to block the entry of the witness' opinion into evidence. It might also be used when a statute, case law, or some other authoritative requirement is necessary before an item or statement may be admitted into evidence.

Not proper scope. A lawyer claims that the cross-examination (or redirect-examination, or recross-examination, for that matter) goes beyond the subject matter of the examination that preceded it.

A BRIEF GUIDE
TO THE COURT SYSTEM

Federal Courts. There are three different levels: the Federal District Court, the Federal Circuit Court (which serves as Appellate Court above the District Courts), and the United States Supreme Court (which serves as the highest federal Appellate Court in the country).

You may file in Federal Court if your case arises out of a federal statute, a United States treaty with another nation, or the Constitution itself. You may also file in Federal Court if there is a civil action with damages exceeding $10,000 being pursued by citizens of two different states. If the same type of case is pursued by foreign nationals, it too can probably be heard in Federal Court, though the full guidelines that apply to all situations are complex.

State Courts. Most municipalities, towns, townships, and cities have what are referred to as Municipal, Traffic, or Police courts; these constitute the first rung on the state court ladder. These courts, regardless of the names assigned to them, usually have jurisdiction over motor vehicle offenses, minor criminal offenses, and, in some states, minor civil actions where there is a claim for money.

The next level usually is the country court level, where civil non-jury or jury cases are heard, as well as criminal trials brought by indictment.

The Appellate Court generally hears appeals from the trial level. Over and above the Appellate Court is usually a State Supreme Court (which may or may not be known by that name), generally providing the last word on all legal issues concerning the citizens of that state -- unless, of course, a federal or constitutional issue is at stake. In that case, an appeal can be taken to the United States Supreme Court, which must determine -- on its own -- whether or not to hear an appeal from the State Supreme Court.

While one set of procedural guidelines exists on the federal level, rules of civil procedure in the state system will vary from region to region. Before you or your lawyer take part in any legal action, you should obtain and review a copy of these rules.

SAMPLE DOCUMENTS
YOU MAY FACE OVER
THE COURSE OF THE TRIAL

The following sample represents *some* of the possible documents that litigants may face over the course of a "standard" trial.

Review these items, but bear in mind that each case is different, and that any questions as to content or purpose of the specific notices you may receive or issue in a legal conflict should be discussed with your attorney.

COMPLAINT AND JURY DEMAND

James Smith, Esq.
1 Broad St.
Anytown, NJ 00000
Attorney for plaintiff

SUPERIOR COURT OF NEW JERSEY
LAW DIVISION
NORMAL COUNTY

Docket No. 12345

COMPLAINT AND JURY DEMAND

Plaintiff,
ANDREW POWERS,
vs.
Defendant,
JENNIFER COLE and
JAMES WILLIAMS, jointly
severally and/or individually.

COMPLAINT AND JURY DEMAND

The Plaintiff, Andrew Powers, residing at 123 Main Street in the City of Anytown, Normal County, New Jersey, by way of Complaint says:

1. On or about January 1, 1987, plaintiff, Andrew Powers, was operating his motor vehicle in a careful, lawful and prudent manner on Main Street, in the City of Anytown, Normal County, New Jersey.

2. At the time and place aforesaid the defendants, Jennifer Cole and James Williams, were operating their respective motor vehicles in such a careless, reckless and negligent manner so as to collide with each other and with the motor vehicle of the plaintiff.

3. As a direct and proximate result of the carelessness and negligence of the defendants as aforesaid, the plaintiff Andrew Powers was caused to sustain serious, painful and permanent injuries, was prevented from attending to his normal activities and occupation and was forced to incur divers sums for medical expenses to effect a cure for his injuries.

WHEREFORE, plaintiff demands judgment against the defendants, Jennifer Cole and James Williams, jointly, severally and /or individually, for damages, interest, cost of suit and attorney fees.

JURY DEMAND

Plaintiff hereby demands a trial by a jury as to all issues.

James Smith
Attorney for plaintiff

DATED: BY:

JAMES SMITH

ANSWER AND RELATED DOCUMENTS

Robert L. Mann, Esq.
2 Lake St.
Anytown, NJ 00000
(609)000-0000
Attorney for defendant, Cole

	SUPERIOR COURT
	OF NEW JERSEY
Plaintiff,	LAW DIVISION
ANDREW POWERS,	MERCER COUNTY
vs.	
Defendant,	Docket No. 12345
JENNIFER COLE and	Civil Action
JAMES WILLIAMS, jointly,	
severally and/or individually.	

ANSWER, JURY DEMAND, CROSSCLAIM,
REQUEST FOR STATEMENT OF
AMOUNT OF DAMAGES CLAIMED AND
COUNTERCLAIM FOR PROPERTY
DAMAGE

     The defendant, Jennifer Cole, by way of Answer to the plaintiff's Complaint says:

     1.   The defendant, Jennifer Cole, admits ownership. The defendant, Jennifer Cole, admits operation, date of accident, place of accident and happening of accident. The remaining allegations in plaintiff's Complaint are denied and plaintiff is left to his proofs.

SEPARATE DEFENSES

1.   This defendant denies violating any duty owed to plaintiff.

2.   This defendant denies being guilty of any negligence whatsoever.

3.   Injuries and damages complained of were the proximate result of the sole or contributory negligence of the plaintiff.

4.   Injuries and damages complained of were the proximate result of the negligence of a third person over whom this defendant had no control.

5.   The percentage of plaintiff's negligence is greater than the negligence of this defendant.

6.   The plaintiff's damages are to be reduced by the percentage of his negligence.

CROSSCLAIM

While denying any liability whatsoever, the defendant, Jennifer Cole, demands contribution from the co-defendant, James Williams, for the proportionate share of any sums that might be adjudged against this defendant in favor of the plaintiff.

JURY DEMAND

Defendant, Jennifer Cole, hereby demands a trial by a jury of six persons as to all issues.

REQUEST FOR STATEMENT OF
AMOUNT OF DAMAGES CLAIMED

TO: James Smith, Esq.
    Attorney for plaintiff

TAKE NOTICE that in accordance with the Rules of Court the undersigned requests that within five (5) days of service hereof upon you, you serve upon us a written statement of the amount of damages claimed in the above named matter.

COUNTERCLAIM FOR
PROPERTY DAMAGE

The defendant, Jennifer Cole, residing at 111 First Street, in the City of Anytown, County of Normal and State of New Jersey, by way of Counterclaim says:

1.   On or about January 1, 1987, counterclaimant, Jennifer Cole, was operating her motor vehicle in a careful, lawful and prudent manner on Main Street, in the City of Anytown, County of Normal and State of New Jersey.

2.   At the time and place aforesaid the plaintiff/defendant on the Counterclaim, Andrew Powers, operated his motor vehicle in such a careless, reckless and negligent manner so as to collide with the motor vehicle of the counterclaimant.

3.   As a direct result of the carelessness and recklessness of the plaintiff/defendant on the Counterclaim, the automobile of the counterclaimant was severely damaged, bent and broken, required extensive repairs, was depreciated in value and the counterclaimant lost the use of said vehicle.

WHEREFORE, defendant/counterclaimant, Jennifer Cole, demands judgment against the plaintiff/defendant on the Counterclaim for property damage, interest, cost of suit and attorney fees.

DATED:_____

Robert L. Mann
Attorney for defendant/
counterclaimant, Cole

BY:_____
ROBERT L. MANN

THIRD-PARTY
COMPLAINT WITH
JURY DEMAND

Theresa McGee, Esq.
444 Mountain Drive
Anytown, NJ 00000
(609)345-6789
Attorney for Third-Party
  Defendant, Robin Levine

Plaintiff,
ANDREW POWERS,

            vs.

Defendant,
JENNIFER COLE and
JAMES WILLIAMS, jointly,
severally and/or individually,

            vs.

Third Party Plaintiff,
JENNIFER COLE,

            vs.

Third Party Defendant,
ROBIN LEVINE.

SUPERIOR COURT OF NEW JERSEY
LAW DIVISION
MERCER COUNTY

Docket No. 12345

Civil Action

THIRD PARTY COMPLAINT

    The defendant, Jennifer Cole, residing at 111 First
Street, in the City of Anytown, County of Normal and State of New
Jersey, by way of Third Party Complaint says:

    1.   On or about January 1, 1987, the Third Party Plain-
tiff, Jennifer Cole, was operating her motor vehicle in a careful, lawful and prudent manner on Main Street, in the City of
Anytown, County of Normal and State of New Jersey.

    2.   At the time and place aforesaid the Third Party
Defendant, Robin Levine, operated her motor vehicle in such a

careless, reckless and negligent manner so as to collide with the motor vehicle of the Third Party Plaintiff.

3.   As a direct result of the carelessness and recklessness of the Third Party Defendant, the automobile of the Third Party Plaintiff was severely damaged, bent and broken, required extensive repairs, was depreciated in value and the Third Party Plaintiff lost the use of said vehicle.

WHEREFORE, the Third Party Plaintiff, Jennifer Cole, demands judgment against the Third Party Defendant for property damage, interest, cost of suit and attorney fees.

DATED:_____   Theresa McGee
                                      Attorney for Third Party
                                      Defendant

                          BY:_____
                             THERESA McGEE

DGR ST—1

ALL-STATE LEGAL SUPPLY CO.
ONE COMMERCE DRIVE, CRANFORD, N. J. 07016

Attorney(s):
Office Address & Tel. No.:
Attorney(s) for Plaintiff(s)

SUPERIOR COURT OF NEW JERSEY
COUNTY

Plaintiff(s)

vs.

Defendant(s)

LAW DIVISION

Docket No.

CIVIL ACTION
INTERROGATORIES

TO:

DEMAND *is hereby made of the Defendant(s)*
for Certified Answers to the following Interrogatories within the time prescribed by the rules of this Court.

1. *State with regard to the vehicle involved, either owned or operated by you at the time of the alleged accident: (a) make, model, year, license plate number and registration number; (b) when last inspected prior to the alleged accident.*

2. *State with regard to the vehicle involved, either owned or operated by you at the time of the alleged accident, whether you were the sole owner; (a) if not sole owner, what interest you held; (b) the names and addresses of all persons having any interest and the extent thereof.*

3. *State the name, address, age and driver's license number of the person driving the vehicle involved at the time of the alleged accident; (a) if other than the owner, state whether the operation was with the owner's permission; (b) whether said person was operating said vehicle as the owner's agent, servant or employee. If answer is in the negative, state circumstances under which vehicle was being operated; (c) whether the person who drove the vehicle holds a conditional license, and if so, what condition; (d) whether operator had any defects of sight, hearing, or other physical or mental disability.*

4. State the destination of the motor vehicle at the time of the occurrences complained of.

5. State: (a) weather conditions prevailing at the time of the alleged accident; (b) condition of road.

6. State with regard to the plaintiff's vehicle, and the vehicle either owned or operated by you, the exact portion of the intersection or highway where the alleged accident occurred; (a) direction of all vehicles concerned and portion of the highway being traveled upon by each during said approach; (b) distance from you when you first observed the other vehicle or vehicles; (c) respective speeds of the vehicles at the time of the impact; (d) position of vehicles after impact with relation to fixed objects; (e) what part of your vehicle came in contact with what part of the plaintiff's vehicle.

7. State with regard to the vehicle involved, either owned or operated by you at the time of the alleged accident: (a) how many feet from the point of impact you first applied your brakes; (b) length of tire or scuff marks caused by your vehicle.

8. State whether the scene of the alleged accident was controlled by traffic lights, signs or police officer; (a) their location in relation to the point of impact; (b) color and changes of signals, if any, which occurred at the time of the occurrences complained of.

9. State the names and addresses of all persons riding in the vehicle at the time of the alleged accident; (a) their relationship to you, if any; (b) their location in the vehicle.

10. State: (a) the names and addresses of all persons known to you to possess knowledge of relevant facts concerning the occurrences complained of; (b) as to such persons who were eye witnesses, state their names and addresses and fix the exact location of each such person with regard to the scene of such occurrences.

11. State as to admissions concerning liabilities of parties: (a) conversations at the time of the alleged accident; (b) exact admissions or statements made, to the best of your recollection; (c) the time and place where made; (d) by whom and in whose presence, giving names and addresses; (e) state whether the above were reduced to writing; if so, in whose possession they are now.

12. State if you intend to set up or plead or have set up or pleaded negligence or any other separate defense as to the plaintiff or any other person; (a) what act or acts of negligence you claim caused or contributed to the alleged accident; (b) the facts upon which you intend to predicate the other separate defenses.

13. State the exact date, time and place, and furnish in full detail your version of the alleged accident.

14. State the names and addresses and area of expertise of any and all expert witnesses, including treating physicians and annex an exact copy of the entire report rendered by each expert or a complete summary of each oral report.

15. State whether the defendant has insurance under which the insurance company may be liable to satisfy part or all of a judgment which may be entered in the action or to indemnify or reimburse for payments made to satisfy the judgment.

CERTIFICATION

I hereby certify that the copies of the written reports or complete summaries of any oral reports of treating physicians or expert witnesses, annexed hereto, are exact copies of the entire written report or reports or complete summaries of any oral report or reports rendered by them; that the existence of other reports of treating physicians or expert witnesses, either written or oral, are unknown to me; and that if such reports become later known or available, I shall serve them promptly upon the propounding party, but in no case later than the time prescribed by the court rules.

I hereby certify that the foregoing statements made by me are true. I am aware that if any of the foregoing statements made by me are wilfully false, I am subject to punishment.

Dated: 19   .

Service of the within (Interrogatories) (Answers) is hereby acknowledged:

on   19   .   on   19

---   ---

Attorney(s) for Plaintiff(s)   **Attorney(s) for Defendant(s)**

Attorney(s):

Office Address & Tel. No.:

Attorney(s) for

Plaintiff(s)	**SUPERIOR COURT OF NEW JERSEY**
vs.	*LAW DIVISION* *COUNTY*
	Docket No.
Defendant(s)	*CIVIL ACTION*
	INTERROGATORIES AND ANSWERS

TO:

Demand is hereby made by the Plaintiff(s) of the Defendant(s)

for answers, under oath or certification, to the following Interrogatories, within the time and in the manner prescribed by the rules of this Court.

Unless otherwise indicated, "merchandise" in these questions refers to the goods and merchandise which are the subject of this suit.

1. State:(a) the full name and residence address of each defendant; (b) if a corporation, the exact corporate name; (c) if a partnership, the full name and residence address of each partner.

2. State in detail:(a) what payments were made by defendant(s) to plaintiff(s); (b) the dates, manner and amount of each payment; (c) if any credits or set-offs other than such payments are claimed, set forth the nature and amounts thereof; (d) attach hereto copies of all checks and receipts pertaining to such payments.

3. If delivery of any of the merchandise is denied, state:(a) which items were not delivered; (b) if notice of non-delivery was given state to whom, when and in what manner; (c) attach copies of any written notices.

4. If delivery of defective merchandise is claimed, state in detail the nature and extent of each defect.

5. State:(a) whether any of the merchandise was returned by defendant(s) to plaintiff(s); (b) what merchandise was returned; (c) the date, place and manner of each return; (d) attach copies of receipts for such returns.

6. If defendant(s) sold, used or otherwise disposed of any of the merchandise, state in detail:(a) which merchandise was so disposed of; (b) the dates thereof; (c) the consideration or price received therefor; (d) the present location of the remaining merchandise.

7. State what amount is owed by defendant(s) to plaintiff(s) on account of the indebtedness upon which this suit is based.

8. State in detail every defense to this suit not already set forth in any of the preceding answers or in the Answer to the Complaint, which will be offered by defendant(s) at the trial of this action, to support any defense or allegation set forth in these answers, attaching hereto a copy of every writing, record or paper forming a part of such proof.

9. State the names and addresses of all persons who have knowledge of any relevant facts relating to the case.

10. State the names and addresses of any and all proposed expert witnesses and annex true copies of all written reports rendered to defendant(s) by any such proposed expert witnesses.

CERTIFICATION

I hereby certify that the copies of the reports annexed hereto rendered by proposed expert witnesses are exact copies of the entire report or reports rendered by them; that the existence of other reports of said experts, either written or oral, are unknown to me, and if such become later known or available, I shall serve them promptly on the propounding party.

I certify that the foregoing statements made by me are true. I am aware that if any of the foregoing statements made by me are wilfully false, I am subject to punishment.

Dated: 19

....

Service of the within (Interrogatories) (Answers) is hereby acknowledged:

on   19   on   19

....

Attorney(s) for Plaintiff(s)   Attorney(s) for Defendant(s)

INDEX

KNOCK 'EM DEAD

with Great Answers to Tough Interview Questions

The interviewer studies his notepad intently for a few seconds as you settle yourself into a chair. The feeling hits you, very quickly, that you are on trial, but before you have time to bolt, the interviewer looks up, smiles (or doesn't), and the trial begins. What *are* you going to *say* when the interviewer asks:

- *What is your greatest weakness?*

- *How much money do you want?*

- *What would you like to be doing five years from now?*

- *Are you willing to go where the company sends you?*

In *Knock 'em Dead*, Martin John Yate gives you not only the best answers to these and many more difficult questions, but the best *way* to answer, so that you'll be able to field *any* tough question easily and get the job you deserve. *Knock 'em Dead* shows you how to:

- *Turn objections into offers*

- *Get interview appointments from almost anybody*

- *Take firm control of a tricky conversation*

- *Knock 'em dead with the Executive Briefing*

Martin John Yate is the Director of Training for the Dunhill Personnel System, one of the largest and most prestigious personnel services in the country. He knows the ins and outs of the job hunt, and has taught people on both sides of the desk how to handle an interview successfully. He has put all of that knowledge into this book in an easy-to-read, instructive style. Born in England, he lives in Sea Cliff, New York.

Bob Adams, Inc.
Boston, Massachusetts

$6.95   ISBN 0-937860-69-7